Suge Knight:
The Rise, Fall, and Rise of
Death Row Records

Suge Knight:
The Rise, Fall, and Rise of
Death Row Records

The Story of Marion "Suge" Knight,
A Hard Hitting Study of One Man, One Company
That Changed the Course of American Music Forever

By Jake Brown

Colossus Books
Phoenix   Los Angeles

Suge Knight: The Rise, Fall, and Rise of Death Row Records—The Story of Marion "Suge" Knight, A Hard Hitting Study of One Man, One Company That Changed the Course of American Music Forever

by Jake Brown

Published by:
Colossus Books
A Division of Amber Books
1334 East Chandler Boulevard, Suite 5-D67, Phoenix, AZ 85048
amberbk@aol.com   www.amberbooks.com

The publication is designed to provide accurate and authoritative information in regard to the subject matter covered. It is sold with the understanding that the Publisher is not engaged in rendering legal, accounting or other professional services. If legal advice or other expert assistance is required, the services of a competent professional person should be sought.

COLOSSUS BOOKS are available at special discounts for bulk purchases, sales promotions, fund raising or educational purposes.

California Love by Tupac Shukur, Andre Young, Roger Troutman, L. Troutman, N. Durham, W. Cunningham. Copyright © 1995 by Joshua's Dream/Interscope, Pearl Music/Warner-Tamerlane Publishing Corp, Ain't Nuthin' Goin' On But Fuckin', Saja Music/Songs Of Lastrada, Stonsee Music.

Cover photos by Ken Nahoun
© Copyright 2002 by Jake Brown and COLOSSUS BOOKS
ISBN #: 0-9655064-7-5

Library of Congress Cataloging-In-Publication Data
Brown, Jake.
  Suge Knight : the rise, fall, and rise of Death Row Records : the
story of Marion "Suge" Knight, a hard hitting study of one man, one
company that changed the course of American music forever / Jake Brown.
    p. cm.
Includes bibliographical references (p.   ) and index.
  ISBN 0-9702224-7-5
1. Knight, Suge. 2. Knight, Suge--Imprisonment. 3. Sound recording
executives and producers--California--Los Angeles--Biography. 4. Death
Row Records. I. Title.
  ML429.K65 B76 2001
  782.421649'092--dc21

                            2001053912

10 9 8 7 6 5 4 3 2 1

First Printing March 2002

Dedicated to James and Christina Brown

Acknowledgments

Thank you first and foremost to Marcy Northrup of the Northrup-Meyers Literary Agency for exemplary agenting and personally for believing in me, Tony Rose and Colossus Books for believing in this project's potential and importance as a story that needed to be told, thanks to the staff at Versailles Records and Big Daddy Distribution, and to the staff at Death Row Records.

Contents

Introduction

Guilty til Proven Innocent

On August 25, 1998, the California Court of Appeals, after routinely considering one of many thousand appeals to criminal court rulings they hear yearly, agreed with a defense contention that their client had been improperly sentenced under the terms of a plea agreement reached three years earlier. The Defense argument was simple but clever: their client had been charged with two felony counts; the Los Angeles District Attorney's office had proposed a plea bargain wherein, in exchange for a no-contest plea on both counts, the felony status of the charges would be reduced to that of a misdemeanor; a nine year suspended sentence was subsequently imposed, with an active probation term of five years.

A year and a half into that probation term, in September, 1996, a Los Angeles district court judge has violated the terms of that plea agreement by ruling that, based on a minor physical altercation the said defendant had been involved with, he had violated his probation terms, and was required by law to serve the full nine year term that had been previously suspended.

The defense in their appeal argued that the District Attorney's office had failed to reduce the felony charges, wherein a judge would have been governed by a much broader array of sentencing options, ranging from probation to the full nine year term. The California Court of Appeals agreed, overturning the nine year sentence and ordering a new probation hearing for the defendant. Given that the defendant had already served two years of the prison term, he would have been ordinarily released with credit for time served. Upon receiving the news, the defendant's attorney remarked that "given the amount of time (the defendant) had been in custody…we are confident that the trial court will impose a new sentence that will allow for a virtually immediate release." Ordinarily.

Unfortunately, the new probation hearing was never set, as ordinary protocol ceases to exist in the Los Angeles legal system when the defendant is Marion "Suge" Knight, founder and CEO of Death Row Records. As it happened, word of the Appeals Court's decision had worked quickly to unsettle the calm that had become certain circles in Los Angeles. A fear quickly set in that ran as low as the gangland streets of South Central Los Angeles, and as high as the California State Supreme Court, who, a year later, mysteriously ruled in a closed-door session that the District Court Judge's nine year sentence should stand, despite the fact that the Appeals Court had clearly ruled the sentence a violation of Mr. Knight's Constitutional rights. The California Supreme Court's ruling made international headlines, drawing an eerie similarity to the media focus that had surrounded the events leading up to the initial revocation of Suge Knight's probation a year and a half earlier, on the night of September 7, 1996.

That night, Suge Knight had attended the Las Vegas title fight between Mike Tyson and Bruce Seldon with Death

Row recording artist and film actor Tupac Shakur. Following the fight, a fight had ensued in the lobby of the MGM Grand Casino and Hotel between long-time Bloods gang affiliate Knight, his entourage (including Shakur, who it later reported was the instigator of the brawl), and a member of the rival Crypts gang Orlando Anderson, wherein Knight and Shakur reportedly participated in a group beat down of Anderson. The altercation was captured on hotel security videos (later the key piece of evidence with which the LA District Attorney's office argued Knight had violated his probation). Approximately 2 ½ hours later, while riding in the passenger's front seat of Knight's BMW, Tupac Shakur was struck by a hail of 13 bullets, including one that struck Knight in the head. Shakur would be pronounced dead five days later at Las Vegas Memorial Hospital, and Suge Knight was taken into custody a short time thereafter based on events captured on the hotel security video.

The nationally televised probation hearing that would ultimately send Suge Knight to prison embodied all the elements of a media fantasy—a celebrity defendant, a politically-motivated prosecution, allegations of corrupt law enforcement, and a court decision that when probed revealed both the depth of Knight's power, the system it threatened, and the lengths to which Big Brother would work to suppress Knight and Death Row Records.

Ironically, the government approached Knight's conquering with the same vengeance that he had applied in his effort to overpower a system that had for years worked to keep African-Americans out of controversial positions of power: "I consider Suge Knight a political prisoner, so whenever anybody from law enforcement says anything (negative) about him, it doesn't surprise me...He is an African American who acquired a great deal of success, and I think that threatened people as a result." In substantiating the opinion of the aforementioned attorney, Milton Grimes, one only need consider the astonishing breadth of the accusations that have been thrust at Knight since his incarceration—rivaling any case of harassment by the government against a minority businesman in recent history.

Highlights have ranged from a joint F.B.I./A.T.F./Justice Department probe into Racketeering, Drug, and Money Laundering charges against Knight and Death Row, to the Los Angeles Police Department naming Knight in late 1999 as a chief suspect in the murder of New York-based Bad Boy Entertainment rapper Notorious B.I.G., wherein Knight is alleged to have masterminded and ordered the murder of B.I.G. from his prison cell. While neither allegation has produced an indictment to date, the police have cited as a principle reason the reluctance of anyone within Death Row's camp to implicate Knight: "You're talking about a tight-knit music community and people involved in this community who have been prone to violence in the past... (and unwilling to talk) out of fear for their lives, out of loyalty to the people involved, and somewhat similar to gang murders."

The aforementioned theme of community has been central to the success of Death Row Records, from its inception and meteoric rise to the top of the Billboard Charts, through the present day. It is a concept that has worked both in favor of and against Suge Knight, resting at the core of his mental outlook on where he sits today, reflecting a peace channeled principally through loyalty. Loyalty to the place and people he feels helped to make Death Row, and on behalf of whose cause he has been willing to advance at any cost, even to that of his own freedom: "The next generation is key. I owe them a chance so they don't have to end up in jail like me...I feel I was taught a lesson...One minute

I'm running a multi-million dollar business, the next I was in prison. But I have paid my debt. I'm a better man…(and) I'm the only one left. Everyone else has sold out. Death Row is the last of the African-American-owned labels."

While prosecutors have sought to use Knight's allegiance to his inner-city community of Compton against him for years—alleging among other things that Death Row Records was founded with a $1.5 million loan from convicted 1980's drug lord Michael "Harry O" Harris, and that while the label grossed over $300 million in sales revenues in its six years atop the charts, it turned no profit in part because Knight funneled much of the money back into the South Central Los Angeles drug trade via the Bloods street gang. Those same government entities have gone even further, accusing Knight of serving as the ruthless overlord to a criminal empire designed in part to fund a personally lavish lifestyle at the expense of Death Row Artists.

Though Knight's criminal record of eight arrests and six probations since 1988 was showcased at his probation violation hearing in 1996 to back the prosecution's claim that Knight was a danger to his community, prominent members of that community came forth at his trial to defend Knight, including Danny Blackwell of LA's Brotherhood Crusade, Rahim Jenkins of Washington DC-based Righteous Men's Commission, and Melba Jackson Carter, a prominent mentor of African American men in South Central Los Angeles. Additionally, onetime Rodney King attorney and Civil Rights activist Milton Grimes argued on Knight's behalf that "…(Black Leaders) see this man as a saviour…He can feed the mind of young people…by (being) willing to change his lyrics…his message." Whether this was a calculated plea designed to influence the trial judge toward lenience or a legitimate acknowledgement of another step in the direction Knight had been intending to take Death Row since day one in open to debate.

As Knight himself would remark to the judge in at the same hearing in support of the latter scenario: "I know I do a lot of good for my community...these people need me." As the media has chosen to focus almost exclusively on the elements of Knight's business approach that compose his notoriety, they have in the process often ignored the repeated acts of generosity Suge Knight and Death Row Records have committed through much of the 1990's in the name of community betterment—including annual celebrations sponsored at $75,000 a pop by Knight for single mothers living in the Compton neighborhood of South Central Los Angeles, whom Knight transports to Beverly Hills for a candle-lit, five course Mother's Day champagne brunch; the annual Thanksgiving Turkey dinner that Death Row sponsored for hundreds of inner-city families who could not afford meals of their own; a service Knight sponsored which chauffeured family members to visit African American males who were serving time in California's penal system when they were otherwise unable to afford transportation costs out of their inner-city neighborhoods; and the hundreds of jobs that Death Row Records provided for African American males, many of whom had gang affiliation with the Bloods, and most of whom have acknowledged would otherwise be engaged in illegal criminal activity to make a living (high-lighted by a custom low-rider shop, Let Me Ride Hydraulics, that employed 15 African American men at a time.)

The consistent blind eye paid to Knight's acts of generosity on behalf of the community he was raised in, and had succeeded legitimately out of, caused the media to largely miss the fact that the collective betterment of African Americans was a regular theme within the organization of Death

Row Records, and central to the end Knight attempted to achieve with the company. Additionally, the media's ambivalence to Knight's acts of good will in the name of more sensational headlines that focused on the methods by which he sought that end are due in part to the fact that Knight never sought out the spotlight in the same way it sought him. Suge Knights' actions during the rise of Death Row Records always followed a clear and consistent rhythm, glamorized by the music Death Row's artists laid over it, and successful to the degree it was solely because of Knight's voracity.

In describing the philosophy behind his approach to a reporter in 1993, Suge Knight outlined his blueprint to success without apology: "The first thing you do is establish an organization, not just a record company. I knew the difference between having a record company and having a production company and a logo. First goal was to own our Master Tapes. Without your Master Tapes you ain't got shit. Period."

A glaring example of Knight's uncompromising approach toward establishing the aforementioned organization lies in the steps he took to free Dr. Dre, his partner in founding Death Row Records, in 1990 from his contract with Eazy E's Ruthless Records. As urban legend recalls the events, later confirmed in a pair of federal racketeering suits filed by Eazy E and manager Jerry Heller, Dr. Dre, who was locked into legalized slavery with Eazy's label, receiving 2 production points an album against 8 platinum albums produced in three years for the label, wanted out of his deal and turned to Knight for assistance. In exchange for release, Dr. Dre agreed to found a record label with Knight managing business affairs, and Dr. Dre managing creative direction.

What followed is reminiscent of the Johnny Fontaine band-leader story from The Godfather, wherein Dr. Dre phoned Eaze E to meet at a recording studio to work out their differences regarding Dr. Dre's contract. Upon arrival, Eazy E was met not by Dr. Dre but by Knight and two co-harts who insisted, backed by the threat of physical force, that Eazy E sign releases for Ruthless Records artists Dr. Dre, DOC, and Michelle. When Eazy E refused, he was not physically harmed. Instead, as legend has it, Knight handed Eazy E a single piece of paper bearing his Mother's address, where Knight insisted his entourage was headed next if the releases were not signed. Subsequently, the releases were signed.

Separating how much of the aforementioned is truth from fiction remains a mystery to date. The results that can be confirmed are as follows: Dr. Dre, DOC, and Michelle were released from their multi-year contracts with no compensation to Eazy E, and two Racketeering suits were filed against Knight and Dr. Dre in Federal court and later dismissed for lack of evidence. Dr. Dre's comments on the validity of the incident have been few if any, and consistent with Knight and Death Row Records' unapologetic approach to conducting business: "As far as I was concerned, he got me out of the contract. "

Jerry Heller, former manager of Ruthless Records' artists NWA, Ice Cube, Dr. Dre, DOC, and Eazy E, who in the past has lamented on the record of coming home to his house and checking under his bed for bombs per Knight's threats, offered only the following when asked how he feels about Suge Knight's actions today: "He's out of my life now..." Heller's sentiment has been shared by more than a few industry personalities who suffered financial and emotional humilities at the hands of Death Row's relentless rise to the top of hip hop throughout the early and mid-1990s. With Suge Knight scheduled for release from Mull Creek State Prison in mid-August, 2001, after serving just over five years of his nine year term, many wonder whether Death Row Records will ever be the super-label it was in its heyday?

A different perspective might seek to measure the latter question in different terms, not in those of the label's commercial heights which ultimately cost Knight his freedom, but rather in terms of the label's resilience through an endless barrage of lawsuits, artist departures, criminal probes, and corporate dissolutions. Why Death Row Records has maintained throughout the past 4 years of Knight's incarceration, it could be argued, is attributable mainly to a label possession that violates the age-old rule of white-owned Corporate Recording Labels—control of Master Recordings.

Because Knight broke down most of the existing barriers these labels had imposed since the 1950's against African American superstars, by insisting on ownership of the label's Masters in its deal with Inters cope Records sealed in 1991, Death Row has managed to survive off the catalog of platinum releases that Knight racked up so diligently in Death Row's hey day. As a result, the label has sold an astonishing 15 million records since Knight's incarceration in 1996. Highlights to this catalog include a co-released Tupac Shakur Greatest Hits package with Jive Records/Amaru Records, which sold 10 million copies, and the less commercial label-loyalist hits like 2000's Suge Knight Represents: The Chronic 2000, which featured no new artist material, and still managed a top 10 debut and went Gold, selling 500,000 copies. Part of Death Row Records' quiet staying power is attributable to its grass-roots fan base, comprised of both inner-city and suburban fans who number in the hundreds of thousands, and who hold a shared belief that Knight is the victim of an over-zealous, media fueled prosecution, designed in large part to tear down Knight and Death Row Records.

The hypothesis is complicated, but valid upon inspection. By conventional label standards, Death Row should be bankrupt and dissolved, yet through community loyalty it continues to survive, despite consistent and targeted harassment by both State and Federal authorities. Reviewing more closely the events that lead up to Knight's incarceration provide substantial evidence that Suge Knight was the target of an at-least partial government conspiracy.

Suge Knight's no-contest plea in exchange for a five year probation term and nine year suspended sentence came as a result of an incident that had occurred three years earlier in 1992, wherein Knight had allegedly pistol-whipped two aspiring producers who had used an phone without permission in the Death Row offices. Though three years passed before the case came before a Judge, because the charge was initially filed as an assault in the first degree, and Knight held two prior felony convictions, the deal proved significant on several levels. Most importantly, because the District Attorney's Office had agreed to reduce the felony to a misdemeanor in exchange for a no-contest plea, Knight was shielded from California's three strikes law. That point alone further substantiated Knight's appeal argument that the Judge had erred in imposing a nine-year term because such a term was based on a felony, not a misdemeanor, which has been pivotal in making the deal attractive to Knight in the first place. As Knight's lawyers had argued, "...their client's no-contest pleas in 1995 were involuntary because they were based on false promises by prosecutors. They argued he should have been allowed to withdraw his pleas, making the terms of probation moot."

Equally important to the plea agreement were the circumstances under which it was negotiated and subsequently executed. While top officials within the Los Angeles District Attorney's office had worked out the terms of the deal, it was later learned that the principle prosecutor who finalized the plea and was assigned to supervise Knight through the probationary term, Deputy District Attorney Lawrence Longo, had developed several conflict-of-interest relationships with Knight and Death Row Records following the sealing of the deal. Judge Ouderkirk, presiding at the time over the deal, called its terms 'unusual', but nevertheless agreed to the plea at Longo's recommendation. The ties between Long and Knight were both of a business and personal nature, and included Longo leasing his family's Malibu Colony beach home to Death Row Records' general council David Kenner for $19,000 monthly, (whereafter Knight is reported to have stayed for days at a time), and Longo's daughter Gina, 15 at the time of the plea, signing a recording contract with Death Row Records for $50,000 (though it was later determined that she never recorded a single demo).

While Longo was subsequently fired from his job with the District Attorney's office and suspended from practicing law by the California Bar Association, the most significant element of this relationship, whether it favored Knight at the time or not (Longo has denied the ties to Knight in any way affected his handling of the case), was the fact that these dealings had come to light at the same time as the Shakur murder, which resulted in Knight being picked up for probation violation.

The mere appearance of impropriety on behalf of the Los Angeles District Attorney's Office in favor of Knight was an immediate headline for the press, and subsequently became a centerpiece of District Attorney-hopeful John Lynch's campaign against sitting District Attorney Gil Garcetti, who was facing a tough re-election campaign. Coupled with the high-profile loss that previous year of the OJ Simpson double murder trial, and the subsequent acquittal of Death Row Records artist Snoop Dogg in his own murder trial, any ruling which favored Knight in his probation violation hearing, given the media coverage, and in light of the connections that had been made between Knight and Longo, would have surely proven disastrous to Garcetti's campaign.

As a result, Suge Knight was made an example of and given the maximum term of nine years, though the Appeals Court would later rule the sentence to be unconstitutionally excessive. Adding an extra element of potential pressure was the fact that, at time of sentencing, the judge who had originally approved Longo's plea bargain was forced to excuse himself from the case, citing the possibility that he could be called as a witness on questions concerning the impropriety of the circumstances with Longo: "In a tense, heated hearing before giving up the case, Judge Ouderkirk suggested that the financial dealings could possibly amount to bribery, extortion, or obstruction of justice, (remarking that) 'they raise at least the specter of criminal charges.'"

Ironically, the Deputy District Attorney who argued on Garcetti's behalf against Knight's request for continued probation was OJ Simpson prosecutor William Hodgman. Whether Hodgman's assignment to the case was an attempt by Garcetti to repair some of the damage from the Simpson loss with a front page victory involving one of the losing prosecutors is open to debate, but Garcetti's motive was clear as Hodgman argued for the maximum nine years. Citing Knight's eight arrests, two prior felony convictions, and six probationary terms since 1988, Hodgman had argued to the judge: "How many bites of the apple does this defendant get?" Ignoring the fact that he had a broad array of sentencing options because of the original terms of the plea, LA Superior Court Judge J. Stephen Czuleger chose instead to give Knight the maximum possible term, painting Knight as a danger to society: "Mr. Knight, you blew it. In the interest of public safety, I cannot put you back on probation."

An important element to exposing the deliberately excessive nature of the Judge's sentence resides in a brief examination of the very action that had caused Knight's probation revocation in the first place. The role Knight had played in the aforementioned scuffle with Orlando? Anderson on the night of Tupac Shakur's murder on September 7, 1996, remains open to interpretation; depending on which side of the table you sat in the court room the following month. What the security video from the MGM Grand Hotel and Casino had clearly depicted was Knight as party to the beat down, wherein his participation consisted of a single kick. The prosecution argued that this action was clearly aimed against Orlando Anderson, the victim, despite the fact that Anderson himself testified before the Judge at the probation hearing that Knight had not assaulted him. In fact, Suge had tried to help him, supporting a defense contention that Knight had gotten involved to break up the melee.

The Judge gave Knight the maximum, to which Knight responded: "It wasn't a nine year kick." Still, with Knight's conviction and imprisonment Garcetti had his redemptive legal victory to the humiliating loss of the OJ and Snoop Dogg acquittals, and he ran on that conviction into his re-election victory the next month.

Though the excessive nature of the sentence Knight received was recognized by the Appeals Court a year and a half later, political pressure was clearly applied thereafter to the State Supreme Court's decision in reversing the order the lower court, when in a closed door session, the Court without explanation upheld the District Judge's original sentence. What did the District Attorney's Office and the State Supreme Court have to hide in reversing the Appeals Court's decision, and why without public explanation of any sort? Did Knight's notoriety run that high or did the conspiracy to bring down Knight's rise to power reach that deep into the unfortunately classic history of overzealous prosecution on the part of the US Court system, both at federal and local levels?

Famed defense attorney William Kunstler was the pioneer of arguing successfully against, and as a result, exposing, the ugly history of the US legal system's oppression of minority leaders who had threatened the control of the white establishment by rising controversially to prominence. Beginning with Kunstler's successful acquittal of the Chicago 7 and spanning through his symbolic representation of the Gambino family mafia crime boss, John Gotti, in his appeal to his 1990 conviction on murdering and racketeering convictions, wherein Kuntsler had argued that Gotti's 6th Amendment right to choice of council had been denied. The appeal was based on Kuntler's argument that Bruce Cutler, who had won two prior acquittals of Gotti via a defense argument of overzealous prosecution at both trials, had been (sneakingly) removed on the prosecution's premise that he might be called as a witness at trial (though he was never called.) Kuntsler made his reputation as the defender of a citizen's right to due process and protection from an overzealous government. The two often went hand in hand in the cases Kuntsler won, and clearly the interplay between the two had existed in Knight's case. The LA District Attorney's Office had violated Knight's due process rights by arguing for a sentence that was legally incorrect by the fact that the felonies had not been reduced to misdemeanors, as promised.

By imposing the maximum sentence when Judge Czugleger should have given Knight much less time, Knight's case fits the classic model of our government's persecution of minorities who achieve controversial positions of power: "I've learned...that many high profile cases, where the (prosecution) has a large stake in winning...law enforcement will go to any extremes to make its case," stated William Kuntsler.

The role that Knight's notoriety has played in at least partially securing his conviction is undeniable; such that not even Knight has shied away from confirming the no-holds-barred approach he took while operating Death Row Records. The media had taken Knight's criminal record and coupled it with the rampant rumors and allegations surrounding Death Row Records to paint Knight into the role of public enemy # 1. Where this image became relevant to the Los Angeles District Attorney's office and its publicly elected head official, Gil Garcetti, rested largely in the perception on the part of the voting public. Though rumors and allegations of violence had surrounded Death Row for years, cataloged both in the headlines and in court filings, none of the accusations had ever stuck.

By the time of Knight's incarceration, highlights of Knight's hits and the District Attorney's misses, included failed racketeering probes, a series of high profile acquittals involving Death Row Records Dr. Dre and Snoop Dogg, coupled with Knight's own criminal record. Suge's criminal record includes a 1987 guilty plea to battery with a deadly weapon; on September19, 1991 a guilty plea to violating penal code 242 for battery; on October, 30, 1990 a no contest plea to an separate battery charge; on December 24, 1990 a guilty plea to disturbing the peace; on December 4, 1991 a guilty plea to carrying a concealed weapon; on November 24, 1992, a guilty finding by a jury in Clark County, NV of felony assault with a deadly weapon; on January 18, 1995, a charge of conspiracy to illegally possess a fire arm; on February 9, 1995, a guilty plea to two counts of assault with a fire arm; and finally, in Las Vegas, NV in 1993, Knight was listed as the 34th defendant in a drug-distribution indictment in which cocaine was transported from Los Angeles and sold in Las Vegas, whereafter Knight ended up with a conviction for gun possession.

In each of the aforementioned cases, Knight served no prison time, but was instead put on probation. The notoriety that grew out of Knight's ability to avoid prosecution for violent incidents, almost all of which had been related to Death Row's business dealings, served only to bolster Death Row Records' image of invincibility. As that image fueled both the label's record sales and belligerence toward the notion of authority, be it corporate or legal, Knight renamed the label in 1995 following Snoop's acquittal and the acquiring of Tupac, "The New and Untouchable Death Row Records." Knight made no apologies for his relentless approach toward expanding the power of his company at any costs, but rarely acknowledged its violent side. This lack of acknowledgment left room for speculation, fueling the press's rumor mill and record buying public's appetite for sensationalism: "The rumors are helpful but not true... They get me additional respect, and this business is about getting the respect you deserve so you can get what you want. I don't worry about all the talk."

One of the principle ironies in the way Knight was villainized for the tactics he chose to utilize in freeing his label from traditional corporate strongholds lay in the fact that those tactics were traditionally utilized by the recording industry to deprive African American artists of their dues for years past. The difference was Death Row seeking to reverse history, principally by distinguishing itself as the first black-owned label to retain complete control of its master catalog. An alternative scenario would show the deal Sean Puffy Combs aka Puff Daddy aka P. Diddy made with Arista Records in starting Bad Boy Entertainment. Under the terms of that deal, Arista retained 50% ownership in Bad Boy, and complete control of the label's master recordings, offering Combs an option to buy the catalog from Arista 5 years into Bad Boy's inception for what Arista determined.

Death Row had rewritten history by defying an ugly tradition that had gone unpunished for years, and had cost African-Americans billions of dollars in royalties. An important element to understanding why Knight's approach in operating Death Row Records was acceptable under the aforementioned circumstances lays in briefly examining the history of independent music from Rock and Roll's commercial birth in the 1950's, largely on the backs of black rhythm and blues and rock and roll artists. Assuming the record industry had accepted Death Row's independence, they subsequently tolerated Knight's actions partially as a result of the aforementioned abuses in years past at the expense of black artists. The premise was then set for Death Row Records to break new ground in not only recouping the lion's share of the profits derived from the sales of the label's all-black roster of artists, but also to defy the age-old practice of depriving those artists of their share of monies due.

Unfortunately, while such a comparative examination highlights the commonality of Knight's tactics on the part of white label owners over the past 40 years, it also serves to expose the downsides to attaining the power Knight did via the approach he chose in operating Death Row. Further, it calls into question Knight's motives in terms of the ends he sought to achieve by those actions. Did Suge Knight seek to better the lives of his artists, or did he abuse the trust his artists placed in him to manage revenues they earned by instead using those profits exclusively for his own benefit? Did Suge Knight proceed with total clarity in the approach he took in operating his business, or did the lines become blurred between what was and wasn't an appropriate instance to employ violent tactics to achieve a desired end? The fact that few dared to question the validity of Knight's actions only served to embolden the mogul, and further empower the label as it sold more records based on the image of invincibility.

Arguably, the principle architect of the history of artist deception and pioneer of Mafioso tactics in the record business is Morris Levy, founder of Roulette Records. As one of the early forefathers of the practice of substituting his name for that of the composing artist as songwriter on publishing copyrights, wherein he received songwriting royalties in place of the actual authors. Levy made no apologies for this thievery, once remarking to an artist who inquired about backend points owed him against a song he had written:" If you want royalty, go to England." There is an astonishing irony in the number of similarities between Levy and Knight, both in terms of their impoverished childhoods, how that background served as a motivation to rise out of poverty at any cost, the tactics both employed to do so, the allegations of artist fraud that both have been charged with, and the ultimate successes and costs to their respective freedom as a result of their allegiances to the code of the street. Both men are products of an impoverished childhoods—Levy grew up in a public housing tenement in the East Bronx, while Knight grew up in the notoriously gang-ridden section of Compton, in South Central Los Angeles.

Both had developed affiliations with organized crime in their teenage years that would remain relevant through their respective professional rises to power in the record industry. Levy's connection resided with the Genovese crime family, whose Godfather Vincent "The Chin" Gigante had been a childhood friend of Levy's since the age of 14. Levy did business with the assistance of and on behalf of the New York mafia for 35 years. Co-owning clubs, including the world-famous Birdland (which he allegedly acquired from mobster Joseph "Joe the Wop" Cataldo), managing artists, promoting concerts, co-owning publishing companies and record labels (including Promo Records, which Levy co-owned with one time Genovese crime boss Tommy Iboli), and enduring constant harassment by the federal authorities. Nevertheless, doing business with Morris Levy was considered something conventional for upward of 40 years:" Morris' gangster ties were never a secret to the record business. To say that few held it against him was an understatement...In the record business, to be close to dangerous men like Levy was to take on some of their attributes and accrue some of their avoirdupois. It conferred far more status than an MBA." Knight too, has retained a life-long affiliation to the LA street gang the Bloods; a connection highlighted no more clearly than in the numerous criminal investigations that Federal and State authorities have lodged against Knight over the past 10 years.

Like Levy, Knight is alleged to have operated Death Row Records in conjunction with and to the benefit of the LA Bloods crime organization, One of the more vicious allegations charges that Death Row Records was in fact founded as a co-venture between Knight and convicted drug lord Michael "Harry O" Harris, who shared the same lawyer as Knight in David Kenner, and who is alleged to have provided $1.5 million in seed money for Death Row Records.

While Knight and Kenner have denied this claim, prison records have confirmed that the two at least had a continuing relationship, with Knight and Kenner visiting Harris at least two dozen times over an eighteen-month period at the California Corrections Institute in Tehachapi, California. While Knight has insisted that Death Row Records was founded based on publishing deals with Sony and other major record labels, he has also cited profits from partial ownership of publishing rights to the 1991 Vanilla Ice hit *Ice Ice Baby* (which he allegedly obtained by threatening to throw the rapper from the thirteenth floor balcony of his hotel suite if he did not sign over partial rights to the song, which Knight alleged was co-written by a rapper who was signed to Knight's management company). Another charge which highlighted Knight's alleged connections to organized crime came to light via a 1996 Justice Department racketeering probe into charges that Death Row Records had been utilized by Knight to launder drug money generated from the Bloods street gang's narcotic enterprise. Knight has consistently refuted this allegation, and to date no indictment has been produced.

Another age-old record industry practice in which Levy and Knight are alleged to have shared in was cheating artists out of royalties. Levy's participation in the aforementioned practice has been confirmed in the past by the mogul himself, while Knight's motives have never been clearly explored or exposed in terms of whether he sought beneath Death Row's lavish surface to cheat his artists of their royalties. While undeniable similarities exist between Knight and Levy in this respect, Levy shared very little of the profits from his catalog with the artists who had produced it, while Knight was renowned for lavishing his artists with houses, jewelry, luxury automobiles, bankrolling multi-million dollar legal bills to keep artists like Snoop Dogg, Dr. Dre, and Tupac Shakur out of jail, and assuming other expenses such as child support payments.

The majority of the allegations against Death Row have come from the label's roster of rappers who are today no longer with the company; citing in part their inability to gain accurate accountings of monies earned and owed them. An examination of Death Row's accounting practices suggests in one scenario that Suge Knight may have been more guilty of excessive spending (often said to include using one artist's revenue to pay for another's bills) and poor bookkeeping (partially supported by the recent revelation that Coopers & Lybrand accountant Steve Cantrock, who is now in hiding, signed a confession stating that he had mismanaged, and in effect, stole $4,500,000 worth of monies owed to Death Row artists, negating Knight from responsibility for the loss) than of any deliberately calculated scheme to deprive his artists of revenues. Conversely, the fact that label co-founder Dr. Dre chose to leave the

label in 1996 with very little in the way of a financial settlement (though he and Suge Knight had been quoted for
years in articles as fifty-fifty partners) suggests that
attempting to lay claim to any of Death Row's assets might
have revealed an underbelly to the success of the label that
Dre decided in leaving to wash his hands of completely.

Morris Levy and business associates like Hy Weiss, pio-
neered the practice of substituting an actual payment of
royalties owed to an artist by offering as a substitute
objects more immediately appealing to the starving eye:
"(Levy) and Weiss (saw) nothing wrong with the practice
of giving an artist a Cadillac instead of his royalties." In the
case of Death Row Records, Knight could be guilty of this
practice deliberately or by default. While it clearly occurred
that artists received luxury gifts in lieu of royalty checks,
very little was ever charged vocally against Knight and
Death Row while artists were signed to the label.

The practice was much more clearly outlined in terms of its
potential illegality in a lawsuit filed against Knight by the
estate of Tupac Shakur, wherein the rapper is alleged to
have generated over $60,000,000 in revenues for the label,
but to have died in debt to the label for approximately $
7,107,186.34: "During the period of his life with Death
Row, Tupac never received an actual accounting of the
monies due to him, (instead)...told that the advances made
by Death Row on Tupac's behalf were more than the
amounts owed him...By advising artists (including Dr.
Dre and Snoop Dogg, both of whom later left the label with
no compensation) that they were 'in the hole', Knight limited the artists' ability to leave Death Row...By failing and
refusing to give the artists an accounting of the funds due
them, (Knight) prevented them from challenging his creative accounting."

While Interscope and Death Row have since settled with Tupac's estate with the award of a large share of the unreleased Master Recordings Tupac recorded for Death Row during his eight months as a label artist preceding the rapper's death, as well as releasing a cash payment of $3,000,000.00 that was paid to Afeni Shakur, the rapper's mother. The immediate payment by Interscope to Tupac's estate prior to their reaching a formal settlement suggests that Death Row Records was guilty of mismanaging artist funds in the vein of Morris Levy. In a related case involving Snoop Dogg's decision to leave the label in 1997 largely based on the artist's claim that the label had stopped paying him and had left the artist with a million dollar IRS debt for unpaid back taxes, Knight's release agreement with Snoop Dogg called for the rapper to relinquish any financial or legal claims against the label.

Further, the rapper agreed to forgo any claim to future royalties against material he had recorded while signed to Death Row Records (including all unreleased recordings), and called for the label to receive a percentage of the gross profits from the next three albums that Snoop Dogg would record for his new label, Master P's No Limit Records, as well as the remaining three that he may record for his own imprint, Dogg House Records. As the question of Knight's motives behind the manner in which he managed, or mismanaged, his artists revenues is central to understanding the larger end he sought to achieve with the success of the Death Row Records, this issue will remain open to further examination and analysis.

Finally, the most volatile link connecting Levy and Knight lies is their shared penchant for resorting to violence as a means to achieve their respective professional ends, coupled with a shared ability to avoid legal accountability

23

when accused or found guilty of the former. For Levy's part, a glaring example of his ability to exercise a violent disposition with no legal repercussions occurred on February 26, 1975 as Levy and his entourage were leaving a Manhattan jazz club, Jimmy Weston's, and were passed by three strangers, one of whom made an explicit comment about Levy's date. Two of the three strangers turned out to be plainclothes police officers, including Lieutenant Charles Heinz, who had made the comment about Levy's girl-friend. What followed was a beating wherein Levy's body-guard held the officer's arms behind his back while Levy punched him in the face until he went blind in his left eye.

Though Levy and his bodyguard, Nathan McCalla, were indicted for felony assault, the case was dropped without explanation prior to trial, and an out of court settlement reached with the officer who had lost his eye. Levy's penchant for violence was tied to his business operations until 1988, when he was convicted on racketeering charges, wherein Levy's FBI-recorded wiretapped conversations with convicted counterfeiter and Genovese crime family member Gaetano "Big Guy" Vastole concerning a business associate who owed the two money included the following exchange supporting the connection that Levy used violence to advance his business interests: " 'Sonny,...I don't like the way this thing is going with this kid, (I'm telling you...I'm gonna put him in a fucking hospital',) to which Levy responded. 'Go out to that place, take over the kid's business.'"

In a similar incident which showcased Knight's tendency toward applying violence in resolving business matters, investigated in its aftermath by the LA District Attorney's office but never producing an indictment as it was settled out of court with the plaintiff for $600,000, Knight is alleged to have lured record promoter Mark Anthony Bell, (who was associated with Knight and Death Row rival Sean "Puffy" Combs, who Tupac, at the time signed to Death Row, had publicly blamed for an incident a year earlier wherein Shakur was shot five times in a robbery ambush outside a studio where he was heading to meet Combs and Notorious B.I.G.) to a hotel suite where Bell was beaten by Knight and associates with Champagne bottles, robbed, and forced to drink from a jar of Knight's urine as the assailants pressed Bell, an associate of Comb's, for the Bad Boy Entertainment C.E.O.'s home address, and that of his mothers. (The latter tactic bears an eerie similarity to the tact Knight employed to free Dr. Dre from his contract with Eazy E four years earlier, in 1991, which the rapper had not agreed to prior to Knight's threatening his mother with physical harm.) Neither incident ever resulted in formal charges against Knight.

Suge Knight could be considered a modern-day reincarnation of Levy, absent the fact that Knight sought, at least in part, to advance the causes of black artists where Levy sought to deny them. In the end, though Suge Knight's approach to dealing with the Corporate roadblocks put in place by people like Levy cost him his freedom, possibly, one could argue, because he suffered from an inability to decipher when his violent disposition helped Death Row's cause and when it acted as a detriment.

Regardless of the fact that Knight may have chosen to blur the lines in the aforementioned respect, he, by his actions, can be credited as being the first African American label owner who successfully freed black artists from the corporate slavery that men like Levy had made a norm. The greatest irony of Knight's current situation is that for all their similarities, it took the government over 30 years before they finally convicted Levy on any charges as they related to his business methods. When they finally did, Levy was found guilty in federal court of racketeering, but never served a day in prison, as a judge allowed him to remain free pending appeal. Levy died two years later of cancer in 1990.

In early 2000, Suge Knight responded with the following declaration to a New York Post reporter's question regarding the imprisoned CEO's current attitude toward his violent past, and what role, if any, it would play in the way he conducted business in the future: "I wouldn't say I'm looking to become a role model when I leave prison, but the violent parts of my life have come to an end." While the parole board, along with an assorted collection of artists and fellow industry executives will be relieved to hear the latter, how the image of the rehabilitated Suge Knight will resonate with Death Row Records' hardcore fan base will determine whether the label survives the new millennium. After all, it is the notoriety Knight generated in the first half of the 1990's that kept Death Row Records alive throughout the second half of the decade. Whether he is personally able to follow through on his pledge of reform while maintaining the hard-edged authenticity of his label's releases is something Knight himself has pondered as his release approaches. In the end, creating a medium between the two will be the ultimate test of Death Row Records' longevity: " People can act like the Death Row concept is over, but to be successful, you have to follow the format we established...(However), this is 2001, I can't do business like its '91 or '92."

—Jake Brown, 2001

Chapter 1

"Sugar Bear"

Suge Knight's undying affinity for and loyalty to his Compton neighborhood in Los Angeles, California draws principally from his upbringing as the only son of a truck driver and home maker in the impoverished and predominantly black section of urban South Central Los Angeles. As a child, Marion Knight, who was nicknamed "Suge" by his mother due to his sweet demeanor, remarked to his parents, that "...one day I'm going to live in a house with a second story and have lots of cars." Years before Knight would achieve the latter with the commercial success of Death Row Records, he would develop a loyalty to the inner city community that would serve as a blueprint for the Death Row philosophy and commercially glamorize, for the first time, the inner-workings of a gang culture that had previously only been hinted at in gangster rap videos and referred to in generic terms on hip hop records.

The (first) example of the latter was captured on NWA's landmark album Straight Outta Compton, in which the group members refer in generic terms to the struggles of surviving in gang-ridden Compton, but largely avoiding specific references to gang affiliations, for instance, with the members of NWA dressing in all black attire in the group's videos in a safer bid for airplay. By 1992, when Death Row Records made its debut, rap had taken on a more commercial tone that seemed to dictate the terms on which it would exist in a commercial market, where it had once proceeded behind the cautious veil of white America's objections.

Where the Parental Advisory sticker had once caused hip hop artists to insert profanity cautiously in their songs, the warning marker now challenged rappers to push the limits of what was permissible to reveal on record. In the case of Death Row's artists, it was the label's gang affiliations and the implied criminal lifestyle that dominated the topic matter on early classics such as Dr. Dre's *The Chronic,* and Snoop Dogg's *The Dogg Father.* Death Row Records was the first label to exclusively advertise gang affiliation with the Bloods gang, wherein the gang's hand signs and colors became a regular fixture in Death Row artist videos. The label even went a step deeper into their exposure of gang culture, shooting their videos on location in the urban gangland of Compton with actual Blood members made regular appearances as extras. As suburban America devoured this image, MTV was obligated to play videos which five years earlier would never have appeared on the network, even after midnight, (let alone starring artists who would later become the subject of video music awards and Rolling Stone covers.)

As the architect of Death Row's gang-friendly image, Knight had cemented his foundation years earlier when he joined the Bloods street gang in his early teens. In building Death Row Records, Knight utilized a combination of street-taught common sense and a chillingly natural penchant toward violent intimidation to establish the label's street credibility on the outset of even its first commercial success with the release of Dr. Dre's debut LP *The Chronic*. The label's loyalty to gang roots was boldly proclaimed in the album's introduction by Dr. Dre: "This album is dedicated to the niggaz who was down from day one. Welcome to Death Row. " And it was. Suge Knight took Death Row's phenomenal first-year revenues based on the success of *The Chronic* and reinvested them not only into the label, but also into the community that he considered fundamental to the foundation of Death Row's success. Emboldening the label's public affiliation with the BLOODS by hiring dozens of the gang's members from his old Compton neighborhood in legitimate positions within Death Row and its subsidiary businesses, including a customized low rider shop located in South Central Los Angeles.

While Knight's actions were beginning to raise the eyes of both critics and law enforcement officials, Corporate-owned Interscope went right along for the drive by, despite the fact that they were part of the target. No one doubted Knight's business savvy, nor dared to question his choice of business tactics, as Death Row Records had brought in $60,000,000 in revenue in the label's first year: "I'm in this game to win. There are no hard-and-fast rules in the industry—no rights or wrongs. As long as you're bringing in the money, they will deal with you, no matter what anybody says." Interscope had foregone any stake in ownership of Death Row's Master Recordings when they sealed a distribution deal with the label, wherein Knight had succeeded in appealing to founders and co-CEO's Ted Fields and Jimmy Iovine much in the way legendary and notorious Led Zepplen manager Peter Garrett had to the band's concert promoters when he had convinced them to take a mere 20% share of the band's gross revenues per show; leaving the band with the remaining 80%. Following the logic that it was better to have 20% of something sure than to gamble anything less, Interscope having any piece of the label that was reshaping the landscape of hip hop forever was proving to be a lucrative gamble.

With the most visionary producer in the history of the genre with Dr. Dre, Suge Knight had a commercial trump card. Even if some argued that he had played from the bottom of the deck by the method he had chosen to utilize in freeing Dre from his contract, the decision was considered sound once the money began rolling in.

Knight's arrangement with Interscope allowed Death Row great freedom in the ways it operated, breeding an atmosphere of invincibility as the label racked up platinum album sales and criminal arrests—a scenario in which the latter owed at least partial credit to the former. Part of Death Row's formula for success came with the authenticity of its stars, who had defied the age-old hip hop tradition of rapping about committing violent acts on record and video without any real life violence or criminal activity to substantiate the claims rappers made. For years, record buyers and members of the media had assumed that hip hop artists were rapping about real life experiences that happened to and around them. Death Row was the first label to confirm and authenticate the reality. A ready example came with the release of Death Row's second multi-platinum debut from ex-convict and Bloods gang member, Snoop Dogg, who turned himself in and was booked on First Degree murder charges the same week his album entered the Billboard Charts, at #1. It would go on to move over six million copies.

Knight thrived in this atmosphere, carefully sculpting Death Row's real-to-life gangster image in tradition and celebration of the BLOODS; putting the gang's customs on display for the media and record buying public for the first time in both parties history. As one reporter remarked, upon entering Knight's offices for an interview with the CEO: that "...virtually everything in the room—the carpet, the cabinets, the sofa and matching chairs—is a striking blood red." Other symbols of Knight's affinity for his gang affiliation included a pair of matching red Rolls Royces that Knight posed with as part of a magazine cover for Source Magazine, a Las Vegas night spot, Club 662 (which spelled out MOB on a telephone pad, or MEMBER OF BLOODS.)

The BLOODS street gang was formed in the late 1950's by Sylvester Scott and Vincent Owens, who lived on Piru street in the neighborhood of Compton, in the South Central section of Los Angeles, California. The gang was initially formed as a means of collective protection against a rival neighborhood gang called the CRIPS, (who were three times the size of the BLOODS at the time of origin. While the CRIPS wore blue to denote affiliation, the BLOODS wore red. As these gangs grew in number simultaneously they began to compete violently for territory, members, and revenues. Gang initiation traditionally occurs between the ages of 10 and 12, wherein for males are "jumped in"; a process which involves surviving a beat down by fellow members and in some cases committing a violent crime on the gang's behalf. Once admitted, Gang members must adhere to a strict code of honor. The rules typically consist of themes including secrecy, lifelong-loyalty, and respect to gang traditions and to older gang members, known commonly as "Original Gangsters" or O.G.'s.

Principle to this code is the time-honored tradition of strict discretion regarding discussion of gang-related matters: "Silence and secrecy are strictly maintained to keep sensitive information about illicit or illegal gang activity internal to the gang and away from parents, teachers, or law enforcement authorities. "Knight exemplified the latter custom years after he had first swore to uphold it when, in 1996, following the murder of Tupac Shakur, Knight in a prison-house *Dateline* interview with Diane Sawyer stayed chillingly silent in response to questions regarding his possible knowledge regarding the identity of Shakur's assailants:" Sawyer: "If you knew any information about the identity of the parties responsible for murdering Tupac Shakur (Knight's best friend and Death Row Records top selling artist at the time), wouldn't you want to tell the police about it?' Knight: 'Absolutely not.' Sawyer, surprised: ' Why?!!', Knight: 'Because I don't get paid to solve homicides.'" Knight's actions were consistent with the BLOODS code of honor, even though his actions served to help the rival CRIPS gang by shielding its member, Orlando Anderson, the LVPD's chief suspect in Shakur's murder.

By the early 1980's, the collective estimate the Justice Department had compiled suggested that there were as many as 50,000 active gang members in the state of California, with the majority concentrated in the Compton section of South Central Los Angeles; among the rival CRIPS and BLOODS gangs. By 1991, the statewide estimate from a decade earlier had become exclusive to Los Angeles County, with a statewide estimate now numbering in the 175,000 to 200,000 range. With the CRIPS and BLOODS numbering as the largest populous within the Los Angeles Gang member estimate, the two gangs contributed in large numbers to the California penal system. The gangs engaged in criminal activities that included robberies, burglaries, felony assaults, drive-by shootings, murders, and the most lucrative of their trades, narcotic trafficking: "By 1983, African American gangs (whose members exclusively compose the CRIPS and BLOODS) (had) seized upon the availability of narcotics, particularly crack, as a principle means of income...CRIPS and BLOODS had established criminal networks throughout the country and capitalized on the enormous profits earned from trafficking and selling of crack cocaine."

Though Suge Knight has been accused for years by both State and Federal authorities of varying degrees of involvement in the BLOODS drug trade, utilizing Death Row Records as a legitimate means to launder drug profits earned by the gang, very few have ever stuck. Only a handful of substantiated connections have ever been established, beginning with a claim by convicted drug lords and BLOODS gang members Michael "Harry O" Harris, currently serving 28 years in prison for dealing cocaine and attempted murder, and Patrick Johnson, also a BLOODS gang member (and operator of one of the largest PCP drug rings in the nation during the 1980's). The pair was alleged to have provided at least $1.5 million in seed money to underwrite the founding of Death Row Records in 1991, (in which he and Knight were purported to be 50-50 partners in the venture.) Media sources have cited the fact that all three men shared legal council in David Kenner as evidence to substantiate the pair's claim against Knight, focusing on the fact that Knight and Kenner visited Harris at least two dozen times during 1991 at the California Correctional Institution where he was housed in Tehachapi, California.

Another purported link suggests that Knight and now-deceased LAPD Officer, Kevin Gaines, and Officer David

Mack (who was arrested in December, 1997 for the armed robbery of $722,000 from a Bank of America on Jefferson Avenue in Los Angeles), both of whom grew up in Knight's neighborhood and as teenagers were members of the BLOODS street gang had worked for Knight in their later years moving narcotics and guns: "(Officer) Gaines had been living with Sharitha Knight, rap star Snoop Dogg's manager and the ex-wife of Death Row Records mogul, Marion 'Suge' Knight,...A Death Row insider (confirmed) that Gaine and...David Mack were confidants of Knights and were frequently seen at Death Row functions." The final, and only confirmed connection between Knight and gang-related drug trafficking activity stems from his being named as the 34th defendant, (along with Ricardo Crockett, a childhood friend and fellow BLOODS member), in a grand jury indictment filed in Las Vegas in 1993.

Crockett was accused of participating in the operation of a drug-distribution ring, in which cocaine was transported from Los Angeles over state lines for sale in Las Vegas by a number of sub-distributors between July, 1992 and May, 1993. The indictment further accused Crockett and associates of robbing other dealers of their money and product. While Crockett ended up being convicted of multiple drug charges, Knight was convicted only of gun possession and sentenced to probation.

Despite the integral role that Knight's affiliation with the BLOODS gang may have played in his formative years, Suge Knight had other, more legitimate interests; principally as a defensive end his high school football team. Suge's parents had always encouraged him to capitalize on his size and talent for football as a means to rise above the poverty-stricken neighborhood of Lynwood, in the city of Compton. After graduating high school in 1983, Suge Knight played ball for a season at El Camino Junior College, where he caught the eye of a recruiter from the University of Nevada at Las Vegas in 1984.

Following his recruitment into the University's team in 1984, Knight played for two seasons through 1986 under the guidance of head coach Wayne Nunnely, currently head coach of the New Orleans Saints. Knight lettered both seasons with the University's team. In 1987, Knight was recruited by the Los Angeles Rams and played a partial season with the team before being injured and subsequently cut. As his college coach Wayne Nunnely recalled, Knight's affiliation with the BLOODS street gang was secondary on the field, though his coaches were aware of his background with the gang: "He wasn't a problem guy at all…You didn't really see that street roughness about him."

Another coach of Knight's from his days with the University of Las Vegas has offered insight into Knight's determination to succeed by remarking that "he played for me and gave me 100 percent, and that's the thing I judge a man by." Upon being cut from the RAMs late in 1987, Suge returned to his old neighborhood and reestablished his connections with the BLOODS, remarking years later in an interview that "it wasn't meant to be, so I moved on." One of the principle pieces of evidence substantiating Knight's relationship with the BLOODS during this period comes via en examination of Knight's criminal record between late 1987 and mid 1990. This was a period which included a 1987 guilty plea to assault with a deadly weapon for which Knight received probation, a guilty plea to battery on September 19, 1990, and a no contest plea a month later, on October 31, 1990 to another battery charge, where in each case Knight received summary probation.

It was during this period that Knight began promoting local Los Angeles-area concerts, and working part time as a Body Guard for R&B acts like Bobby Brown. He was becoming social with N.W.A. group members including Dr. Dre. As Knight became more familiar with the inter-workings of the record business, he also began managing artists, including a rapper who had co-written the Vanilla Ice hit *Ice Ice Baby* but had not been given credit for his contributions to the song. In a move reminiscent of the late Morris Levy, (who got his start in publishing after founding a music publishing company in an attempt to collect unpaid royalties), Knight founded his own publishing company, aptly titled SUGE Publishing, and went about collecting his artist's share of royalties from rapper Vanilla Ice: "After forming a small music publishing company, Knight almost got the shaft...when it came time to get paid...off Vanilla Ice's huge, albeit briefly...successful debut album... 'But I didn't let that happen...You can get fucked real quick in this industry if you don't know what's going on.'" The incident that allegedly followed in which Knight collected the royalties owed his company is hip hop legend, and served to launch Knight's reputation as Hip Hop's most notorious and influential CEO of the next decade.

Chapter 2

The Psychology of Intimidation

An F.B.I. psychologist and instructor at the Bureau's training academy once classified intimidation to his class of new recruits as one of the most effective means of eliciting information from a suspect during an interrogation. Ironically, the same federal agency has investigate Death Row Records and its CEO Marion "Suge" Knight repeatedly over the past ten years for allegedly utilizing that very tactic to advance the organization's business interests. Many of America's top business schools have cited intimidation as a fundamental element of practicing competitive capitalism. More importantly, however, is the root of intimidation as it exists in the work place, that being centrally located in the heart of the human ego.

While large egos drive many of the modern world's most successful and prominent business personalities, it is also at the root of a majority share of the stress, conflict, and in many cases, abuse that can exist as readily as productivity in a business environment. The fact that many successful business personalities also the owners of cosmic-sized egos has traditionally has made it very difficult for anyone, especially a business owner's employees, to point out when ego's cup hath excessively overrun, principally because the ego-holder is incapable of hearing criticism of any kind on the matter. The result of this denial can be devastating in the long term to the stability of a business, as much as it can be responsible in the short term for a business's successful growth: "People with runaway egos often are in denial about their behavior. They see themselves as tremendous employees or managers with few, if any, faults. (In this light) there's no question that the human ego is at the root of a number of problems in business everywhere...The ego can force managers and owners to make decisions that feed the ego. Those decisions might be good for the individual's self-image, but bad for the business in some way."

Not surprisingly, Suge Knight majored in Business while attending the University of Las Vegas on a football scholarship, where he was at the very least exposed to the latter theory. Whether Knight applied more of his street or textbook education in the subject of intimidation, or more probably a combination of the two, as part of the methodology by which he operated Death Row matters less, as a means, than in the end result he achieved because of it. As a club-patron with no affiliation to Knight once summarized matter-of-factly when Knight passed him on a dance floor, "That Suge Knight ain't no motherfuckin' joke."

From his earliest days as a body-guard following his release from the Los Angeles Rams football team, Knight sought to project an image of (someone to be taken seriously), working as a bodyguard to Bobby Brown in late 1989, and later for seminal rap group N.W.A., where he befriended future-partner Dr. Dre. Even then, Knight had an ambition which seemed competitive with that of stars he was paid to protect, such that he soon moved from bodyguard to manager, where he readily employed violence as a means of achieving his desired end, no matter what moral or legal or emotional codes it violated in the process. In exploring what motivated Suge Knight to resort repeatedly to violence as a means of achieving a desired end without any apparent regard for the affects his actions had on the victims, or for the possibility that it could one day have adverse implications for him personally, or for his company, one has to examine the psychological factors which lay as the roots of a violent mental foundation, including the pre-existing psychological disposition toward an acceptance of violence as a norm, and more importantly, a fundamental disregard for the impact that such a disposition can cause in its effects.

The latter has been cited time and again in both allegations and convictions against Knight for committing acts of violence in the course of conducting business. The sort of desensitized violent approach that served as Knight's hallmark in Death Row's heyday has seldom been explored in terms of its psychological underpinnings, possibly out of an inherent fear, or lack of desire or willingness on the part of Knight's employees or artists to attempt to understand their leader's motivations, preferring to accept, or in slang terms, roll with, the fruits that Knight's tactic often bore, caught up in the moment, without a timekeeper.

The only parties keeping the clock on Knight were the government entities who sought time and again to derail Death Row with legal charges that would not only expose the negative side of the lifestyle the label and its community celebrated, but more importantly, hold its purveyors accountable for the adverse impact that their lifestyle ultimately had (one of Death Row's favorite means of avoiding such accountability was to settle with the victims financially out of court in exchange for sealed testimony). Because the legal system was unable to formally acknowledge Knight's recklessness in the form of a conviction, he had no reason to pay attention either. More importantly, because his legal invincibility appeared to run on forever as yet another current in Death Row's seemingly endless river of wealth (via record sales which glorified the lifestyle), Knight's employees, artists, and entourages, had no reason to regard the violence that regularly surrounded and consumed them as anything strange, or out of the ordinary, and as a result, wrong.

Part of the reason for the aforementioned accepted norm on the part of those who surrounded Knight laid in the fact that most of Death Row's employee base had come from the same neighborhoods as Knight, and were therefore already predisposed to an acceptance of the violence that defined much of the gang lifestyle, and to the code of silence that prohibited a discussion, let alone an exploration of the psychological aspects of why such a mentality was acceptable.

Mental health professionals have traditionally identified many of the behaviors displayed by Knight in the course of operating his business as consistent with those of psychopaths, "(who are) characterized by egocentricity, shallowness, manipulativeness, deceitfulness, selfishness, and lack of empathy, remorse, or guilt."

While Knight has clearly displayed symptoms of most of the latter, a sister characteristic of Knight's personality which laced most of his interactions with business associates and artists was an ability to 'sweet talk' anyone, such that as a child it earned him the nickname "Sugarbear" from his mother, later shortened to 'SUGE'. What made Knight's approach lethal to opponents was that he coupled Death Row's violent interior with a charismatic exterior soaked in a wealth that Knight knew how to spread around to the right parties in the right ways—to his artists in the form of lavish houses, automobiles, and jewelry, to his corporate label partners in the form of record sales, and to his legal protractors in the form of high-priced legal defenses. Through all of the latter, Knight maintained an iron-fisted control over almost every element of his reality, employing the majority of the aforementioned psychopathic characteristics in some form, and collectively in what could be argued as a classic psychological model termed *executive functioning*, wherein every move is calculated around a single goal of control.

The flaw of this approach comes in trying to balance a means with an end, i.e. at what cost is one willing to pursue a goal, or maintain success once it has been achieved? It is here that the deficits of seeking to maintain such complete autonomy begin to arise, residing principally in the links that have been established between psychopathic behavior and the deficits of executive functioning. As one medical professional phrased it: "Like a busy CEO, your brain is constantly making long-term plans and carrying them out. This activity requires a host of cognitive processes, known collectively as 'executive functioning', that allow you to set goals cognitive processes, known collectively as 'executive functioning', that allow you to set goals, make and modify mental models of actions, organize your activity, focus your attention selectivity, and avoid impulses and distractions that could sidetrack you from accomplishing your aims."

In defining the connection between an individuals' pursuit of goals and reckless nature that can arise from seeking to do so at any cost, the doctor went on to establish the association between antisocial behavior and executive functioning, concluding that "...there is a robust and statistically significant relation between the (psychopathic or) antisocial behavior and executive functioning deficits."

Medical professionals have gone on to identify the connection between psychopathic behavior and executive functioning deficits as (mediated) principally by the frontal lobes of the brain. The latter is one of the key factors psychologists and psychiatrists have cited time and again in the study of psychopaths and their tendency toward violent criminal behavior, specifically that uncovering the roots of the connection between the two lay an examination of what they have characterized as a disturbed frontal lobe function: "...research suggests that the prefrontal cortex, an area of the brain involved in long-term planning and judgment, does not function normally in psychopathic subjects. Studies have since suggested that such an impaired functioning of the brain's frontal lobe can be linked conclusively to a number of pathological behaviors: "...Abnormalities of the frontal and temporal lobes can predispose an individual to antisocial or violent behavior."

In attempting a study of any of Suge Knight's potential frontal lobe malfunctions, it may be appropriate to briefly establish in more elaborate terms what characterizes psychopathic tendencies, and where Knight's behaviors have been consistent with such a label. One psychiatrist, Robert Hare, who specializes in the study of psychopaths, defines the breed as "...interspecies predators who use charm, manipulation, intimidation, and violence to control others and to satisfy their own selfish needs." In breaking down each of the latter components to Dr. Hare's definition, there are countless documented examples of actions Knight employed to support such a characterization. For example, *Charm* is (summed up) in Knight's nickname, Suge, from the prefix SugarBear, wherein his mother once explained that he could charm anyone into conforming to his order. Tupac Shakur, according to many of his friends, family, and business associates, was entranced by Knight's generosity, in awe of his power, and eager to impress his mentor upon release from the custody of the New York penal system and into that of Death Row's.

By Tupac's own account: "When I was in jail, Suge was the only one who used to see me. Nigga used to fly a private plane, all the way to New York, and spend time with me. He got his lawyer to look into all my cases. Suge supported me, whatever I needed. When I got out of jail, he had a private plane for me, a limo, five police officers for security." Kevin Powell, a writer for *The Source* hip-hop magazine who had interviewed both Knight, and Tupac Shakur numerous times over the course of the early 1990s, described the relationship as one in which "...Shakur, who grew up fatherless, was drawn to the charismatic Knight as a father figure."

Manipulation was a hallmark of Knight's approach in dealing with his artists in the course of managing their business affairs. Ready examples include Dr. Dre's recent settlement with (PriceWaterhouseCoopers) over alleged mismanagement of his bank accounts while a partner with Suge Knight in ownership of Death Row Records, specifically that the accounting house allowed Knight and his associates to loot millions of dollars from the Grammy-winning producer's accounts to finance the label's lavish lifestyle at the ultimate expense of Dr. Dre's financial stability. As both Knight and Death Row chief council at the time David Kenner pleaded Fifth Amendment protection against self-incrimination, the accounting house settled for Dre to the tune of approximately $15 million dollars. In another example, numerous examples of financial misappropriation were cited in a lawsuit filed against Knight and Death Row Records by the Estate of Tupac Shakur, cited as 'fictitious expenses' including examples wherein "...In August 1996, Tupac was charged $2,965, Check No. 16754, for an American Express bill incurred by Knight's wife. In fact, Knight allegedly now owes American Express in excess of $1.2 million; Tupac was charged more than $120,000 in rental costs for a house in Malibu, which was actually occupied by Death Row chief council David Kenner; On June 13, 1996, Tupac was charged $2,700 for child support paid on behalf of Nate Dogg, another Death Row performer, Check No. 15404; Tupac was charged $57,600 for rentals paid by Death Row in connection with an apartment located at 10601 Wilshire Boulevard. That apartment was not occupied by Tupac, but by other Death Row artists."

Examples of Knight's tendency toward the characteristics of *Intimidation* and *Violence* go hand in hand, and are best exemplified in what proved to be Knight's most notorious instances of utilizing a violent approach of intimidation which resulted in the launch of Death Row Records in the fall of 1991. The first involved Knight's threatening Eric "Eazy E" Wright with harm to his mother if he did not sign releases for Ruthless Records' artists Dr. Dre and DOC (subsequently Knight obtained the releases, and founded Death Row Records with Dr. Dre. Wright later sued Knight and Dr. Dre under federal racketeering statutes.) The second instance involved white rapper Vanilla Ice (Robbie Van Winkel) who, depending on which of his accountings you believe, was hung off the thirteenth floor of a hotel balcony following his refusal to sign over partial rights to the hit "Ice Ice Baby" (which a rapper under Knight's management had co-authored), or was verbally coerced into signing the publishing release. The rapper first told a reporter from Dateline in a 1996 interview following Knight's incarceration that his life had been threatened in a manner consistent with the hotel balcony version of the story.

In a 1999 VH1 Behind the Music variation, Van Winkel watered down the latter account to fit an account of someone who was clearly still haunted by the incident, but not seeking to so vocally implicate Knight in a manner as extreme as a murder threat: "He threatened me, but not verbally. He showed at places and showed me he knew where I was at all times. He came in my room one night and he had some papers and, I'm not stupid, I figured out what was going on, so I signed them. You can look at it like I was an investor in Death Row Records without a return on my money. I made a lot more money off this music thing than I ever expected, so I looked at it as a price I had to pay. This happened nine years ago and I don't have any hatred toward Suge and I hope he doesn't have any toward me." He went on in another interview to acknowledge the possibility that his life could still be under threat, lamenting that "...I wish it would have never come out, but here we are on the other side and I'm just trying not to be a target. I don't need a target on my forehead."

Dr. Hare has cited egocentricity as one of the principle characteristics of those with psychopathic tendencies, implying an impulse to "cold-bloodedly take what they want and do as they please, violating social norms and expectations without the slightest sense of guilt or regret." Rooted in the latter characteristic is an (fundamental) need to control, specifically an inability to tolerate insubordinance, which Knight was notorious for. An appropriate example of the aforementioned being the incident which resulted in an Assault conviction that put Knight on the probation term which ultimately sent him to prison via its violation, in which Knight pistol-whipped a producer who had used Knight's office phone without permission, remarking to the assaulted man "Listen to me when I tell you to do something!"

While Knight's action, by his own account, was a response to a defiance of his order, it was an overreaction by any civilized standard, and further indicative of a characteristic that psychiatrists have identified in psychopathic criminals wherein the traditional processes in which words or actions prompt emotions is defective, resulting in a *fear imagery* of the way they are being disobeyed, perceiving it as a larger threat than it ever truly is: "The psychopath's inability to respond in a normal manner to fearful imagery helps to account for the reckless, impulsive lifestyle...and to explain why verbally oriented approaches of treatment... are so notoriously ineffective with this population." Scientifically, medical researchers have argued that such behavior "supports a relationship between frontal-temporal dysfunction and certain types of antisocial (or violent) activity."

Interestingly, in exploring the balance that Knight maintained between running a multi-million dollar business while dealing mentally with the arguable existence and impact of the aforementioned psychopathic traits on his decision-making processes, an element of the human psyche which exists among millions of Americans who deal daily with underlying psychological disorders emerges. Whether Attention Deficit Disorder (commonly dubbed ADD), or Obsessive Compulsive Disorder (OCD), many of our nation's most successful and productive citizens face private battles with medical conditions which they have learned to live with over the course of their lifetime, wherein they have had to learn to adjust situationally to the disease's existence.

For example, many adults who live with Obsessive Compulsive Disorder take a short series of daily breaks, sometimes in 15-minute intervals, to experience exposures to a given compulsion for the purposes of getting it out of their system. The baseline of this treatment is an acknowledgement of the disease's existence, which is largely absent in the world of the psychopath, who traditionally seeks to hide his tendencies from greater world: "In one prison study involving 54 prisoners assigned to low- and high-psychopathology groups...(wherein their) skin, cardiac and facial responses to fear imagery and neutral sentences (were recorded)...The psychopaths reported having the same responses upon hearing the fear-imagery sentences as did the non-violent prisoners—even though the tests showed that they were reacting differently. The researchers (determined) that non-affective memory operations were intact with these individuals...(and) consistent with the 'mask of sanity' psychopaths present to the world." That Knight on one hand was able to conduct himself in a civil manner in corporate board rooms while wielding a savage hand behind the closed doors of his inner-sanctum in the presence of company employees, who were for the most part gang-members already predisposed to Knight's flair for violence, suggests another behavioral trait consistent with that of a psychopath's.

Another characteristic of the psychopathic mind is an extension of the aforementioned egocentricity, namely a need for immediate gratification, which implies a natural abandoning of the cause-effect rationale, i.e. the long term consequences of an impulsive reaction. Medical professionals have cited this trait as 'Now-Oriented Thinking', again consistent with the theory linking the behavior with damage to the ventromedial prefrontal cortex, wherein choices are made with immediate gratification or reward in mind, and the concept of any consequence or punishment largely out of mind: "('Now-Oriented Thinking)…is comparable to the real-life inability to decide advantageously, especially in personal and social matters (in which) an exact calculation of the future outcomes is not possible…(These people) are generally insensitive to future consequences, positive and negative, and thus their behavior is always guided by immediate prospects, whatever they may be."

Out of this mentality, a sub-symptom emerges wherein testosterone-driven thrill seeking is stimulated, and acts committed without regard for long term consequences, and in the interest of immediate reward. The latter characteristic is consistent with a variety of criminal behaviors, and has been cited time and again by medical professionals as the driving factor behind the committal of many violent crimes: "Sensation seeking in adult males has consistently been linked to adult antisocial (and psychopathic) behavior".

Part of Knight's disposition toward this characteristic, notably in his inability to consider the potential consequences of his actions the night of the MGM beat down, could arguably root in the common acceptance on the part of African Americans that death or downfall is somewhat imminent in the culture. Certainly this mentality was preached in gang doctrine, such that there were rules covering the subject which acted as a contingency plan of sorts, that being the code of silence, wherein members do not talk out against each other regarding illicit or illegal activities. Suge Knight sat in prison for four years not because someone testified against him, but because he was caught on surveillance tape, acting out a moment's impulse that was based on years of mental training to live in the moment according to a code of survival that was in many ways contradictory in an long-term sense. Arguably, Knight had lost his ability to differentiate between acting on his psychopathic tendencies and reading the potential consequences that could result.

Both Knight and Tupac Shakur embodied the latter mentality, and it's end result was the loss of Shakur's life and Knight's freedom. The actions of Knight and Shakur that night clearly followed a pattern of psychopathic traits the root of which is an under-appreciation for life which runs rampant through urban African-American population, and accounts for almost (70%) of the violent offenders in the US penal system. Source writer Kevin Powell, who interviewed Tupac Shakur several times during his time with Knight and Death Row, supported the notion that Knight and Shakur operated from a 'Now-Oriented' mentality as Shakur believed his death was imminent: "One thing Tupac said to me—I remember me saying to him 'Why don't you just be careful?', and he said 'There's no place like careful. If its time to go, its time to go.' I think that's sad. In black America some people are just waiting for death...I think if there's anything we can learn from Tupac, its like, man, you cannot live your life that fast and that hard and that recklessly without thinking through every decision you make...I am amazed at how much (black) people just don't care."

In this way, Knight is no different from any of the sect of his cultural environment who are mentally predisposed to live life expecting to die at any moment, and in subsequent interviews which occurred during the course of his incarceration, has not sought to paint himself as anything else, supporting the argument that his mental disposition is consistent with that in many regards of a psychopath's: "I could strip down naked in (prison) and show all my (gang) tats...People know who I am and who I am down with. One thing about bein' a savage its that you stay that way. When I went to jail, it was because I was involved in something. Its not like I was standin' by and not doing nothin'."

Most importantly, however, in qualifying Knight's egocentricity as a dangerous element of his personality, which ultimately cost him his freedom, is an examination of what defines ego psychology, specifically the concept of the *business ego*—whose characteristics may have ultimately played a principle role in fueling Knight's psychopathic tendencies to the point of self-destruction, i.e. incarceration, even while he built a recording empire as a result of that very drive. As Knight was an admitted work-a-holic, in some cases staying up for three days at a time before he would sleep, his mental equilibrium was arguably imbalanced by the combination of the mental pressures associated with managing a multi-million record label and the physical and mental rigor that was associated with such a responsibility.

Psychologists have traditionally associated sleep deprivation and work-related stress as factors in a psychological imbalance that affects a variety of behavioral areas in the brain, notably including impulse control and the ability to react rationally in stressful situations. A key physical affect of both sleep deprivation incurred in connection with work-a-holism is loss of blood to those parts of the brain which directly affect balanced and mentally healthy decision making: "…reductions of blood flow to the prefrontal cortex may correspond to executive dysfunction and poor impulse control, and that temporal lobe dysfunction may result in violent behavior." Coupled with Knight's repeated instances of almost certain violent overreaction to stressful situations, exemplified in his decision to pistol whip a producer for talking on his office phone too long, was an ego the size of a platinum record population.

The legend surrounding Knight's ego and fiend-like addiction to complete autonomy within any situation to which he was party has persevered to this day. It dictated the terms on which Death Row competed for territorial propriety in hip hop in the early and mid 1990s, and has not been absent Knight's mental constitution through the present day, principally in Knight's inability to identify any of the elements of his violent disposition in Death Row's heyday as anything abnormal. Quite to the contrary, he prides himself in many cases on the latter approach for the lengths his label and legacy has traveled as a result of it.

The ego is traditionally defined as the "part of the brain that contains the basic functions (which are innate and develop through maturation and interaction along biopsychosocial factors) essential to the individual's successful adaptation to their environment." The most important elements of ego development are those of drive, the quality of interpersonal relationships, hereditary and constitutional endowment, the impact of immediate environment, sociocultural values and mores, socioeconomic conditions, social and cultural change, and social institutions. In Knight's case, the most crucial element of ego development centers in that the ego not only mediates between an individual and his environment, but also is the mediator for internal conflict among various aspects of the personality.

Because Knight was raised in an less than desirable socio-economic conditions, i.e. among the urban working class, in a gangland neighborhood where membership to the aforementioned organization was essential to a sense of security and survival, and where violence and crime were accepted elements of reality, Knight's value system was skewed toward a permanent empathy for the population that resided in those conditions even after he had economically risen above them. As such, Knight never chose to view the world, or approach its challenges, from any other perspective than that of someone fighting his way out of what was very much a form of economic slavery. When Suge was free of those chains, he took his whole neighborhood along for the ride, gang affiliation, and so on. That he on one hand had a mental loyalty in disposition toward the ghetto and its plights, and on the other had to function as a corporate executive and play to the implied elevation and separations in class and outlook, a natural mental paradox in perspective existed.

Knight had no problem playing Robin Hood, but he couldn't shoot the sheriff. Instead he had to resort to allegedly robbing his own artists to make the whole facade work. That one part of Knight's ego was gratified by indulging his community while indulging himself equally gratified another, Knight operated in a constant state of mental conflict. The only area of his operation in which he seemed resolved was his ready reliance on and acceptance of the use of violence as a means to achieve his desired mental ends, no matter how many of them there were hanging at one time. In short, Knight had a lot to manage, and his ego was a centerpiece to the balance in all the balls he was jiggling. That he had internal conflicts and contradictions was as natural as being human, and the fact that he handled it as masterfully as he did for as long as he did speaks volumes in terms of any analysis of his motives, and how they may have naturally contradicted one another: "The social environment shapes the personality and provides the conditions that foster or obstruct successful coping. The nature of cultural, racial, and ethnic diversity as well as differences related to sex, age, and lifestyle must be understood in the assessment of ego function."

Knight's principle paradox might have been trying to topple the barriers he broke down. Trying to mix two worlds, one of institutionalized poverty and one of new-found wealth that had no real history or handbook on how it was to be best managed. The things that Suge Knight had down were how to break new artists, generate money and spread it around, and intimidate people into not asking questions that held any real answers or long-term implications.

From one perspective, everything Knight accomplished in Death Row's heyday was very temporary because it happened too fast for him to ever really take stock or root. As a lawsuit fueled by the estate of Tupac Shakur pointed out in documenting the disorganized by design fashion in which Death Row operated, "Death Row's accounts were always overdrawn, and their checks would have bounced in almost every case were it not for (Interscope, Death Row's distributor) accountants." Evidence has surfaced in Federal investigations into allegations that Death Row in some capacity was a front for Bloods gang-controlled drug operations that Knight had a large piece of. Death Row's shady financial dealings has to some degree been irrefutably proven by the very fact that almost every major artist on the label has had major financial problems at of one kind or another due to Death Row's accounting regularities. When Tupac Shakur died, he was deeply in debt despite having generated over $70,000,000 in record sales for Death Row in the 9 months he was signed to the label. Dr. Dre and Snoop Dogg have both settled civil suits with Price Water-House Coopers for allegedly mismanaging both artists' accounts while they were with Death Row by allowing the label to loot their accounts for millions of dollars that have never been accounted for. Both suits were subsequently settled for around $15,000,000 respectively. Other artists, like Kurupt of the Dogg Pound was forced to file for bankruptcy a mere two years after his group's album went double platinum.

During this same period, Suge Knight, David Kenner, Death Row's general counsel, and a handful of other Death Row employees were quickly becoming multimillionaires, and to date, are the only members of the organization who have remained financial solvent based on how their respective financial situations were structured around label earnings in its heyday. Additionally, Death Row invested hundreds of thousands of dollars back into the inner city communities of Compton, in some manners legal and others allegedly illegal. It could be argued that in some minds, reinvesting Death Row profits into the Bloods drug trade was investing money back into his neighborhood, since the drug trade has long been counted as one of the more lucrative occupations for black males in inner city neighborhoods. Either way, Knight's conflicted loyalties clearly played a central role in his ultimate conquering.

Arguably, Knight's ego propelled him to attempt to accomplish too much for himself, his artists, and his community.

The role his ego played in the latter is significant, as it still drives him today in what he aims to do with Death Row Records as he is released from prison. In an interview conducted in the Spring of 2001 from Mull State Creek Prison, Knight spoke eagerly of his intention to return to his helm as Death Row's chief operating officer, but did so with a chilling calm when discussing his peace with the actions that had gotten Death Row to its place in hip hop's history books, and he himself incarcerated: "Its like my grandmother said, 'Whatever hand your dealt, you have to deal with.' You can't justify what goes on in life." Such acknowledgement suggests that Knight is mentally indoctrinated to and programmed by his code of the street to a point where he might not ever rehabilitate from it. What he does seem to have achieved is a deeper perspective as to why he is where he is in relation to his own role in the circumstances that got him there.

The fact that Knight is not in denial regarding his actions is less important than the reality that he readily justifies by referring to prison as something of a social norm for his race, and for himself. Perhaps Knight prefers to remain in touch with his violent nature because he considers it an edge that is fundamental to basic survival. To that end, those psychopathic traits that both elevated and to some degree, depending on which perspective you are looking from, adversely affected Knight, are still very present in his present-day mental constitution: "I feel real safe here because I know my environment—I know what I'm dealing with. Its like the devil you know is better than the one you don't."

This makes one wonder whether Knight's parolees, current and former business associates, and some might argue, the general public should fear his release for the fact that prison may not have freed him at all of his old ways. Knight has hinted both ways on the matter, stating on one hand that "whatever I needed to learn, I've learned. I know I'm wiser, smarter, more disciplined, stronger, and more spiritual. I've grown for the better. I don't stay the same; I don't thrive on the negative", while on the other seeming to relish the still ever-present intimidation that the reality of his impending release seems to (cause): "They don't send a nigga who's wearing shiny suits and hanging out with Martha Stewart to jail (referring to longtime rival Sean 'Puffy' Combs). Who he a threat to? I'm the nigga people are afraid of…When I hit the bricks, its all mine."

In further bolstering the notion that incarceration is a natural part of being an African American of the type Knight claims to be, i.e. 'a ghetto nigga from Compton', Knight has aligned himself with an unfortunate social reality which plagues many of America's African American inner-city males: "You comin' to prison, regardless if you did something big or did something minor. There's no way you could be off the block, and hang out, and don't come to the penitentiary…If you a guy that really hangs out, really from the neighborhood, sooner or later you gonna get crossed up. Its sad, but its true that, as far as, no matter what prison I go to, Im'ma have a gang of home boys there. If I go to college, I might know one person there from my neighborhood. The thing about it is, the worse the prison, the better it is for me, for the simple fact that, lifers, and guys got a gang of time, those most generally my homeboys."

Clearly Knight views himself as one among the aforementioned population. The fact that is does works to further bolster to argument that he in many ways is beyond rehabilitation in terms of his psychopathic tendencies. His resolve to affect any change seems to come with discussion of his generation's youth. He has never made an effort to remove himself from his urban foundations, referring to himself time and again in interviews as a 'ghetto nigger', but in virtually the same breath, speaks of young African American children as though they were his salvation: "The next generation is key. I owe them a chance so they don't end up in jail like me. I would never bring harm to a kid. Society paints their own vision; they believe what they want to believe." This quality in Knight's personality is one of his more endearing ones, that of his sacrificial side. He makes no excuses for his actions, viewing them as a natural affect of the environment around him.

What is extraordinary about what Knight seeks to accomplish from his experience in prison, as a result of bettering his own situation upon release by regaining his position at the peak of hip hop, is to use that position and the wealth of experience supporting it to self-sacrificially to help others grow beyond where he feels he himself is capable of. In this regard, Knight, while at peace with his disposition and its effects, seems to display a subconscious insecurity or self-doubt regarding his ability to grow beyond it.

That Knight has, on some levels, has accepted his role in the circumstances that landed him in prison is fundamental to the principle of facing consequences, which many psychologists have cited as a first step to rehabilitation. Conversely, Knight is very quick to defend those same actions as necessary, and cite his punishment as excessive at his sentencing hearing in 1996 stemming from the MGM Grand beat down of Orlando Anderson, Knight remarked to the judge after his sentence was handed down: "It wasn't no nine year kick." Perhaps he views the consequences of his actions not as unjustifiable for his own life, but for those of his children, and for the lives of the children who buy his artist's records? Knight has supported this perspective to some end in discussing his plans for Death Row in the millennium as a potential catalyst for real change: "I don't want to talk about the past because we can't change it. We have to move forward and give these new kids the opportunity to reach their own goals. I want to enlighten them and make them entrepreneurs." Perhaps it is then permissible to accept the manner in which Knight approached building his organization by not justifying it, but at least seeking to understand it as the way Knight was conditioned to deal with obstacles.

Another perspective might hold Knight a bit more accountable, acknowledging that what he did was wrong by most social standards, but forgiving his actions in the long term on the grounds that he has paid his debt to society. The latter leaves open the possibility that Knight could resort to those tactics again to have his way, however, given how closely his actions will be monitored by both state and federal authorities, and the fact that Death Row has survived in large part on the oxygen of Knight's own resilience, this scenario seems unlikely to unfold.

Still another perspective, and one of the more supported ones, suggests that Knight took the necessary steps he felt he needed to free his company to grow from the corporate chains that had imprisoned the potential for progress in the African American community for years at the hands of white oppressors, accepted the consequences of those actions, both positive and negative, and feels at peace because he knows he won't again have to resort to violence because of only the shadow of intimidation it seems to have indelibly left on the world of hip hop: "People can act like the Death Row concept is over, but to be successful, you have to follow the format we established. This is 2002; I can't do business like its 91' or 92'."

The goal in exploring Knight's psychopathic tendencies is not to blame him, but to understand why he chose the path he chose in employing those tactics, and at what costs? On one hand, he clearly has long-term goals for Death Row Records as a catalyst for the black community. One the other, he has long employed an unapologetically egocentric approach to operating the label which irrefutably served selfish interests. Justifying his violence on some level is acknowledging Knight's mental disposition as a result of his background: "I can still go to any ghetto in the world, anywhere, and instantly be at home."

Assuming Knight won't change in what he regards as that most basic skill set, he seems determined to affect the next generation of urban youth, ideally shedding the identity of "ghetto niggaz" by building a more positive self image for the children and their mothers who are growing up in that environment now. Death Row has already established a long history of community charity, notably in the neighborhood of Compton, California, where Knight was raised. As he spoke about in one interview describing annual Thanksgiving Dinners Knight sponsored for years for single mothers and their children: "Every year I do, every year that I was on the streets, and one year after I was incarcerated, I would do a mother's day dinner for all (my neighborhood's) single mothers at the Beverly Hills Ritz Hotel. Reason I would do that for the mothers is so they could bring their kids, and know somebody care about them. See, I really did it for the kids because if mothers on Mothers Day, if they don't have nobody to give them no roses, and buy them no gifts, they gonna be grouchy. They might be more grouchy toward the kids, like you know...

'You look like your daddy, your daddy ain't no good.' So I would give them long stem roses, and baskets, and a great big dinner, and we would have performances...and (all our artists) would intervene, and get out there (in the audience) and sit down, not to sign autographs, but to actually give them hugs, and take pictures, and anything that's positive for the kids, that's what I'm all about." Knight has continued his commitment to this goal while in prison, most recently by donating $21,000 from his jail cell to rebuild a Sacramento, California, playground for children from low-income families (including the replacement of a jungle gym with carousels, swings and monkey bars) that was destroyed by vandals, an incident he learned of while watching the news.

As he speaks with reporters about Death Row's future involvement with community betterment, he does so with an optimism that could only arise out of someone with true purpose toward the cause, and in Knight's position, with a real understanding of the potential impact his position can have, and the responsibility that comes with such an influence: "Its time for the younger kids now...I'm not the bad guy that I'm made out to be. When you take a stand on life in America, do things you way and own your own, that can be scary for people...I want to enlighten (kids) and make them entrepreneurs."

Knight's commitment to children ranks him not as a monster, as the media has so often sought to portray, but rather as something of a conflicted individual trying to maintain dual loyalty to positive and negative elements of his fiber which consist of the streets that raised him. In other words, Suge Knight is a human being, and in this light, we can begin to understand that he has as natural paradoxes as we all do in one form or another. His happen to be amplified

Chapter 2. The Psychology of Intimidation

by a number of unique factors, including the obstacles he overcame with the success of Death Row, the media attention that success brought, and the ultimate challenge Knight faced from both Corporate and Government factions who sought to continue the age old practice of dividing and conquering African American progress before it could really be made.

Death Row succeeded, and Knight paid the ultimate price for that success. Much like a captain going down with his ship, Knight has always been the first to take punches for his label, and seems content with that role, possibly because of the greater potential he knows it can offer for his community's next generation: "Its like as far as prison. Everybody (in my neighborhood) glorify prison, say you know 'If you come to prison, you can do work outs, you can lift weights, you get to do this, you get to do all these great things as far as hang out with your homies.' Then they took the weights. But you still can work out. But at the same time, they don't get the who scenario where one year can turn to three years, three years can turn to life. Lotta guys come to prison, their woman run off and leave them. Lotta guys come to prison, people in they family pass, and they can't attend the funeral. Lotta guys might get a tattoo and get aids. There's just certain things, and its sad, and the kids really gotta snap out of it. Kids gotta really wake up and say 'Prison ain't for me. I wanna wake up and do something better than come to prison."

Chapter 3

The Snitch

Those Who Know Don't Tell;
Those Who Tell Don't Know

Suge Knight has long reviled snitches. He inspired an equal hatred among Death Row loyalists, and required it of all those affiliated with the organization, via confidentiality agreements, threats, and Attorney-client privilege in the case of chief counsel David Kenner, who was in essence Knight's partner in operating Death Row.

From early childhood, Knight had been indoctrinated into the culture of silence regarding tell-tailing, even in cases where it worked to his own detriment: "The truth is, if a guy take millions of dollars from you…either you a punk, or you a snitch for telling on him, for saying something about it. You can't have it either or. Either you snitching about something you shouldn't be telling about, if its true. And if its not true, and they took the money you a punk. So you got your choices, what you wanna be? You wanna be a rat, or you wanna be a punk?...Or you wanna sit back as a man and deal with it. You know, if that was me, and somebody did that situation to me, I would deal with it as a man...I (definitely) wouldn't be a snitch."

Prior to his formal induction into gang culture and the implied allegiance to a lifelong code of silence regarding gang-related activity, Suge Knight as a child had been psychologically prepped by his parents to view snitching as the worst form of dishonor amongst men: "I think it most of all, it's how you grew up. I was fortunately blessed to have my father, and my father still around...You gotta be a man. Start off as a young man, then you become a man. And you know, as far as that whining, and making excuses, and complaining, that ain't gonna do no good. And telling is definitely something you don't do. If you outside playing with your friends, and they might be older, and you run and say 'Hey, I'm 7 years old, and they 14, and they took my ball.' The first thing my Pops would say is 'Look boy, don't be no telltale. Get your butt back out there and get your ball back.' And I think that that guidance, that father-figure is very important. Cause if you look at a lot of people who do a lot of telling, and a lot of crying, and be snitches and stuff, they mostly didn't have they father's presence around...(When I was a kid) snitching on somebody would get you in trouble...When I was young, I got whoopings. I think that I deserved those whoopings. I didn't get whoopings, I got ass-whoopings. You know, I was a boy, I was all boy. I wasn't effeminate, I was all boy. So by me being all boy, I broke windows, I did stuff to cars. And you know, my peoples wasn't rich. So when I broke a window, and that means an extra hundred dollars (to fix the window) a month that they depended on that money for something, I got an ass whooping. I think my whoopings was to tough, that, like today, kids can call child services on them right? If I had called child services on my people, they still be in jail doing time, but I deserved every one of the whoopings."

Even in the midst of Tupac Shakur's murder, Knight would abide by his code of silence when he refused police requests for him to share any information he had that might help in solving the murder. In one chilling instance, which occurred during a prison-house interview on *Primetime Live*, shortly following the Shakur slaying, a reporter asked Knight if, had he any information that could help the police identify Shakur's assassin, would he share it with police, he responded resolutely in kind: "Absolutely not...Its not my job. I don't get paid to solve homicides. I don't get paid to tell on people." The problem is that such a position doesn't make immediate sense when revealing information could have helped police in solving the murder of Knight's best selling artist and someone he called his best friend. To understand its logic, one must understand the roots of such a mentality, specifically, as it relates to Knight. In citing the absence of maternal fathers in the upbringing of many of the inner city's African American youth, gang membership has been cited as a principle role in many cases in substituting the role of a father figure in providing fundamental guidance. That Knight had the benefit of his father employing the same mentality as the BLOODS gang code of silence in raising his son only served to further enforce that ideal as a permanent part of the mental constitution he would abide by in adult life.

That same mentality ran rampant through the majority of Knight's entourage of fellow gang members, current and former, who clung tightly to the code of silence. A ready example of the latter is found in the days immediately following the murder of Tupac Shakur, Death Row's best selling artist, when the Las Vegas Police Department found it nearly impossible to gain any cooperation from the large entourage of Death Row affiliates who had been in the procession of cars that witnessed the murder: "Throughout the investigation, police say, witnesses have uniformly refused to cooperate. The detectives were frustrated from the very beginning, stunned by the number of witnesses who claimed not to have seen the assailants, or anything else for that matter. The witness statements were pretty similar, 'I didn't see nothin'. I didn't know noboby. I wasn't even there.' Lieutenant Wayne Peterson commented…(As another officer,) Sergeant Kevin Manning agreed. 'It's the code of that mentality. They just don't care.'"

In expanding on Knight's potential role as a witness, and his refusal to assist police with their investigation into the slaying, police were further frustrated because Knight was not only their primary witness, but also a victim of the assault, which should have enhanced his interest in helping the police solve the murder: Lieutenant Wayne Petersen, (commented regarding Knight) "He's obviously a prime witness in this, also a victim, and we've gotten no cooperation from him. We believe we know who's responsible for this. The problem we have with this case is we don't have anyone willing to come forward to testify to it. The gangster…mentality that they don't…talk to police is definitely hurting this case." In citing their belief that they had identified a suspect, the police were referring to rival Crips gang member, Orlando Anderson, who had been the subject of the MGM beat down involving Knight, Shakur, and the rest of the BLOODS-affiliated Death Row entourage earlier in the evening.

Ironically, in the aftermath of the shooting, many of the same entourage who were riding in Shakur and Knight's BMW-led procession that night who had refused to assist police with any potential identifications of the assailants were willing to share with officers their distress about the shooting. The extent to which the murder had affected Skakur's entourage would be vividly and violently illustrated in their gang-style retaliation a few short months later. However, on the surface, Knight's camp maintained an chilling mask of indifference: "I had to calm the bodyguards down" said Bicycle patrol officer Michael McDonald, (who had arrived at the scene a few minutes after the BMW was stopped), "They were saying, 'Man, we have to go to the hospital with Pac.' They were freaking out. Their friend had just been shot."

The fact that members of Death Row's entourage were willing to share their remorse with police over the shooting, but not information regarding anything they might have witnessed in conjunction with it, further illustrates how powerfully the gang land code of silence that Knight and his affiliates abided by had become engrained in their collective psychology. In essence, it controlled the process of mental prioritizing as it occurred. More importantly, however, was that their obedience to the rule of silence clearly demonstrating that Knight's BLOODS gang operated not only by its own code of values, but that its members had been trained in how to be cognitive of that code at all times; never letting down their guard long enough to be human beyond the few words that Shakur's bodyguards had been willing to share with police.

It was a programmed response, designed wholly to maintain the integrity of the aforementioned code. More importantly, their willingness to abide by this code of laws was reinforced as a system that worked when, a short time later, the consequences associated with violating that code kicked into effect. In May, 1998, Orlando Anderson, widely believed to be a key party to Shakur's assailant, was gunned down by gang members in what had proved to be the culmination of a series of retaliatory exchanges in the aftermath of the gang-related Shakur murder, which had been rooted in a rivalry between CRIP Anderson and a member of the BLOODS in Death Row's entourage the night of Shakur's murder.

As one report at the Tupac fansite, Hitemup.com, summed up the exchange and subsequent series of slayings: "It started when Travon Lane (Tray), Kevin Woods, and Maurice Combs, Mob Pirus Bloods, were at a Foot Locker at Lakewood Mall. They were approached by three Southside Crips, and Orlando Anderson (Baby Lane) stole Tray's Death Row medallion which happened to be a personal gift from Suge Knight. On the night of September 7th 1996, Suge, Tupac and Travon Lane were at the Tyson/Seldon fight in Las Vegas. While leaving the MGM Tray noticed Orlando Anderson and pointed him out. Tupac stepped up to Orlando and said 'You from the south?', then punched him in the face knocking him on the ground, after which Suge and the Deathrow camp proceeded to beat him. Later that night, Tupac was shot and killed. There is (a myriad) of evidence which suggests that it was, in fact Crips that were responsible for the death of Tupac. The police report names Southside Crips member, Jerry Bonds as the guy who drove the Cadillac in which the bullets were fired from. There was a source that told the Compton Police Department that at Club 662, he heard Tray say that the shooter was Orlando's uncle Dwayne Keith Davis (Keefee D). Orlando Anderson was arrested by Compton police on October 2, 1996 and held for questioning, but they couldn't find any substantial evidence to link him to the murder and (he consequently) was released. The following week erupted in gang violence between Crips and bloods in which many people were murdered. On September 9th, 1996, on East Alondra, a man who Las Vegas police said may have been in the Cadillac, was shot in the back. On the 11th, Bobby Finch, who Compton cops said may have also been in the Cadillac was gunned down on South Mayo at 9:05 am. Two Bloods were shot and killed by an assailant who fled on foot. On May 29, 1998, Anderson and his friend, Michael Reed Dorrough, pulled into the parking lot of Cig's Record Store,...in Compton... Tempers rose and a gunfight erupted. Orlando and the Stones were all fatally injured. An informant told police it was connected with the killing of Tupac."

From a gang member's perspective, it could be argued that a series of rules had been put into affect to maintain the foundations of an operation, and those rules had been strictly adhered to and justice subsequently served accordingly. If so, the result of the Shakur murder in its aftermath only served to reinforce the necessity of and success achieved by adhering to such a code, no matter the adversity a gang member might be faced with, (including prison time in Knight's case as a result of the incident.) No matter how the Shakur murder impacted its gang-affiliated participants, one universal commonality to all parties involved was their vow of silence toward law enforcement.

The root of the aforementioned code of silence is best explored in a brief examination of the history of organized crime, which LA street gangs are in essence a variation of. There are territories, ranks, and clearly rules which govern membership. The most important validation of the BLOODS and CRIPS as bonafide organized criminal entities lay in the fact that their respective members are unified in their adherence to the universal rules which have existed for almost a century in the United States, and for hundreds of years in native Italy and Spain, where organized crime finds its roots. According to the traditional Mafia rules of conduct, the vow of silence, or Omertà, is a sacred code of silence, the violation of which is punishable by death. Ironically, in line with what Knight refers to as a masculine quality, Omertà was a reference in the old Italian country as a term for behavior consistent with that of a man. In many ways, the Organized Crime and Street Gang definitions of Omertà are one in the same, characterized by "non-cooperation with authorities, self control in the face of adversity, and the vendetta in which any offense or slight to family must be avenged, no matter what the consequences or how long it takes (Abadinsky, Mafia 14). The mafia code of Omertà also requires absolute silence about mafia activities and absolute obedience to hierarchical mafia authority. Failure to obey the Omerta oath could result in punishment in the form of bodily injury or even death." A mafia or gang member, once sworn to abide by this rule among a number of others, was required to obey a lifelong allegiance to Omertà, or code of silence.

To Knight, violation of this oath represented betrayal in a much broader sense, and was defined by a broader set of parameters. In Death Row's family, to speak out against the label, let alone to leave it, even in the case of Dr. Dre, who did so in conjunction with an agreement to give up all financial interests in the label, and left largely because of disagreements over the violent culture that consumed its image, was in a sense ratting on or betraying the label by walking out the lifestyle and affiliations it implied. Tupac Shakur, faced a similar dilemma, according to friends and family members who were close to the rapper, in the days immediately preceding his death in Las Vegas. Shakur publicly allied with Knight, proclaiming in one late August, 1996 interview with *Vibe Magazine* that "I'm a (Death Row) soldier...(referring to himself as 'capo' and Suge as 'Don')...Me and Suge will do business together, forever." Privately, however, many have claimed that Tupac desired to leave Death Row, but that his principle hesitation was a fear of Knight's reaction. Shakur had first acknowledged the impact of Knight's street reputation when he signed with Death Row in late 1995, and in the same statement, had flaunted rhetoric which seemed to fit ideally within Knight's definition of life-long allegiance to the Death Row family: "Me and Suge...we're a perfect couple...He rides like I ride...Before, niggas wasn't scared of me...Now I...get respect. Cause motherfuckers is scared shitless of Suge."

As Death Row's fast lane lifestyle complimented Shakur's rapid-fire tounge and image as a hellraiser, some, including his mother, Afeni Shakur, have suggested that near the end of his life, Tupac had grown weary of the real-life version of his gangster image that was rampant in Death Row's world. Though he had technically fulfilled the written terms of his jailhouse contract with Knight, he had signed another deal in the process that was not negotiable in terms Shakur could come to face: "'If Tupac had left Death Row...it would have been worse than devastating—it's an insult. It's a public slap in the face (to Knight). It is not tolerable. I've made you and you're going to leave me? And six months after Dre did it?' In another culture...people sue you' (according to one music industry executive who worked closely with Dr. Dre and Death Row)."

Knight has publicly adopted a 180-degree difference in opinion on Tupac's attitude toward his affiliation with Death Row Records, specifically regarding and vehemently refuting any assertion that Shakur ever had any intention of leaving the label:" If you'd asked Tupac that question that was he planning on leaving Death Row, he definitely would have cussed you out…Tupac loved Death Row. Tupac loved me. I loved him. I mean, Tupac took Death Row to the next level…My main goal is fulfill Tupac's dreams. And Tupac would definitely never want the music to change…. So we'll keep it the way he would like it. I feel like that it's my job to make sure all Pac's dreams is fulfilled, and he stay alive, and keep Death Row alive. I'm not gonna go and say, "Well, just 'cause it's a little crazy in this world, so, I'm gonna sit down somewhere." I'm not gonna sit down nowhere. I'm gonna walk the pattern, talk the same talk, fulfill all his dreams."

Even the police have their own rule of silence, popularly referred to as the "blue wall of silence" which is designed to discourage police from testifying against rogue cops. The only infiltration that law enforcement has been able to establish into the mafia and gangland code of silence has come via informants, who typically are arrested for committing gang or mafia-affiliated crimes and are spared prosecution and given immunity to testify against fellow members for committing criminal activity they themselves may have been witness to or involved in or work simultaneously for both the police and their criminal organization in the capacity of a spy, or 'rat or snitch' as mafia and gang members popularly label such individuals.

Knight has publicly condemned the notion of snitching time and again, but has himself cited the effectiveness of snitches as tools for law enforcement in infiltrating gang and organized crime activity: "Guys on the streets, you know, if they informants, or snitches, they more important to authorities on the streets than in prison." Ironically, some investigations have attempted to link Knight with the Genovese crime family through his lawyer, David Kenner's, connections to criminal defenses of its members in the 1980s. Knight's representatives have responded in kind that "(Suge) wouldn't know a member of the Genovese crime family if he tripped over him." Knight has also used his disgust for snitches to target and refute 1980's drug lord Michael "Harry O" Harris's contention that he provided $1.5 million in seed money for Knight to found Death Row, and was cheated out of his share of label profits.

In addition to ridiculing Harris's contentions as ludicrous and unfounded, Knight has gone on to use Harris as an example in illustrating the fundamental flaw in a snitch's or informant's effectiveness, going as far as to cite it as a psychological flaw in what Knight views as a true man and loyalist's constitution: "You don't have to take my word that their lying. As far as the Mike guy…this guy has told on almost every drug dealer, lied on them, Columbians and anybody else just to try to get freedom. Then he turned around and lied about Death Row to try to gain his freedom, which in a way, to me, is more sad and desperate…You do the crime, you do the time, and suffer the consequences…When I first found out about (Michael and Lydia Harris), they said they owned Rap-A-Lot Records… These are the same people who say they paid for Denzil Washington and made him the actor he is today and took care of him and his wife with drug money…You gotta realize one thing: the law works all the way around…He's a rat, and I don't like rats."

In painting Harris as desperate, Knight sits in the same place Harris does. The irony in the way Knight has chosen to handle his sentence, versus that of Harris's method, is that Knight can speak with a clarity informants never experience, i.e. a peace with their actions and consequences that only comes with the type of lifelong allegiance to the code of the BLOODS that Knight has adhered to. It could be argued that informants display a psychological discomfort on some level, conscious or otherwise, with the course of their lifestyle and the implications of its result as they are forced to disavow it by disclosing the type of secretive information they are required to in the course of testifying. Most snitches, however, have selfish motives, principally in avoiding long jail terms, and are not as morally conflicted.

Knight's discipline earns him, to some measure, an integrity in terms of his resolve to do his time with some dignity, i.e. as a man. In this light, he clearly views snitching as something less than masculine, and has had no problem challenging the manhood of his (accusers), whether they are informers, like Harris, or former artists who have since left Death Row and lodged allegations against Knight: "Anytime anybody away (incarcerated), it give a person an opportunity to say things and do things, and I understand what people would like to say, and would like to do…But I think as a man, anything you say once, you gotta be able to say twice. And Imma respect you, if you can say it twice. If you gonna speak bad about somebody, and you gonna put accusations on somebody, be able to sit down, and look him in his eye, and say 'Yeah, I said that, I did that.' And you know, and everybody else know, that those things don't happen. And that's the difference between being a man…being a rider, and being a coward."

In this way, Knight's analysis of an informant is as a traitor, or anyone who speaks out against him while he's down, thus expanding into a wider examination of his belief that the record industry in some ways, conspired against him, possibly not by putting him where he is in prison, but by doing little to assist him while he has been in jail. That lack of assistance, Knight has rationalized as betrayal in the family, where after his incarceration, the weaker members of his family became vulnerable to manipulation from competitors, and were lured away.

Worse, because Knight feels he has taken the brunt of the punishment for actions he took in defense of his artists and family, he clearly feels that the blame should not be his alone: "If (one of my artists) had a problem, it was a Suge Knight and Death Row problem. If I was with whoever, if someone was going to do something, do something to Dre, or do something to Snoop, they know they would have to go past me to get it done. And I wouldn't allow it because Death Row was a Death Row family. And those situations, a lot of those actions, are me being loyal to the people I'm around, and got me in trouble. But I didn't cry about it, I didn't complain about it, and the minute I came to prison, everybody was (relieved). 'He's gone, we can do what we want to do.' And you know, you look at those situations, it's like with Snoop's case; I don't have nothing against none of those guys, but if you look at it, this guy was going to go to jail for 25 years to life for murder, and…I wasn't late, I wasn't late to put up almost $5 million in attorneys fees, I wasn't late to have, when he was scared to go to court, to have 50, 60 guys escort him in the court room so he wouldn't be beat up. Alls I did was help the guy. If they feel I did something wrong by doing that, ok then, I'm guilty of that…If I'm wrong for that, I'm wrong, but I look at it like, If I'm with you, I'm with you. There's no such thing as in-between, either you with me or against me. If we on the same team, I'm gonna do what I can to always help you."

To make matters worse, by Knight's account, it was his own extended family, that being Interscope, Death Row's distributors, who stole many of his most prominent artists, including Dr. Dre, who formed his own label, Aftermath Entertainment, upon parting ways with Knight and Death Row Records in 1996, where Knight clearly feels there was a betrayal of loyalty: "I don't have nothing negative to say about Interscope, at the same time, when Michael Fuchs from Time Warner, offered me $80 Million and to build me state of the art studios to leave Interscope and go strictly with Time Warner, I turned it down. Because I started with Jimmy and Ted, but if you ask, 'What have they done for me since I been incarcerated, ain't nobody sent me even a pair of shoes, or a book of stamps, so I guess (they) don't understand the laws. I know they…took some of my artists, took some of my producers."

Interscope's record executives might argue that pursuing Knight's artists following his incarceration worked to the benefit of those artist's careers as Knight's imprisonment prohibited him from directly managing their careers. This is logical from a strictly financial perspective, but not from one where party loyalty is put in the gang-affiliated terms Death Row had come to be defined by. Knight's claim that Interscope had maintained a consistent loyalty to his label is contradicted to a large degree by the fact that Interscope severed ties with Time Warner after the distributor came under fire for releasing the type of violent and gang-friendly rap that Death Row became famous for, glorifying in their releases. This allegiance was principally motivated by the fact that Death Row, under Knight's guidance, generated upward of $100 million a year for each of its first four years as a corporation. That Death Row's creative direction was helmed by Dr. Dre (who has been credited universally as the godfather of the Gangster rap genre) and the label's artist stable included Tupac Shakur (who had a long affiliation with Interscope prior to Knight's signing him directly to Death Row) and Snoop Dogg (who proved to be the biggest hip hop sensation of the first half of the 1990s), served as lucrative incentives to tolerate Knight's open gang affiliation and questionable business ethics in operating Death Row.

That Interscope tolerated Knight's violent business disposition only worked to encourage its existence, and further embolden the label in its quest to become rap's premier recording outfit, bringing in more revenue for its parent company. When Knight's criminal record, in conjunction with that disposition, caught up with him, ultimately disabling him from being able to continue as Interscope's principle breadwinner, Death Row's viability became crippled. The fact that Interscope could have potentially lost millions of dollars by continuing its affiliation with the label following Knight's incarceration doesn't, according to his mentality, matter in the face of the principle of loyalty.

Even their dissolution as Death Row's distributor doesn't seem to bother Knight as much as what he views as their passive-aggressive approach to first, stealing his marquee artists, and secondly, doing nothing to help keep him out of jail. He has illustrated the latter point most vividly in describing Arista's support for Sean "P-Diddy" Combs when he had faced his own sets of serious criminal charges. Most recently, in December, 1999, Combs had been charged by New York police with felonious possession of a firearm and bribery in conjunction with a Times Square shooting. A conviction on one or all of those charges could have resulted in serious jail time for Combs and dramatic profit losses for Bad Boy Entertainment's parent company, Arista Records. However, a year earlier, in 1998, Combs had been charged with Battery in connection with the beating of an Interscope record executive, wherein he had ultimately received a light sentence due to his distributor's intervention on Combs' behalf.

Worse, Knight has implicated Interscope as a participant in defending the Combs in the wake of his Battery charge, when the Bad Boy CEO had been Knight's most bitter rival for much of the 1990s: "If Puffy (had still been) with Clive Davis, he wouldn't be going through this ordeal. If you recall, Puffy was right, Steve Stoute (the Interscope music executive Puffy assaulted) was wrong. When Steve portrayed Puffy in a way he didn't want to be portrayed (in Nas's 'Hate Me Now" video, where Puffy objected to the scene where he was hung from a cross), Steve should have respected him and took it off the video. But he didn't. So Puffy goes over with his friends, expresses himself (assaulted him with a wine bottle), and Steve snitched on him. All of a sudden, Clive Davis calls Jimmy Iovine, and said 'Okay, look, yo' guy over there is telling on my guy. Now my guy making me money, and owes me money (Puffy has an open $50,000,000 line of credit with Arista for use in operating Bad Boy Entertainment), so tell yo' guy (Stout) to drop the charges.' So Jimmy says, 'How will I do that?' 'Well, give him a position. Tell Steve Stout he's a President or Vice-President. Give him a title even though it don't mean nothing.' And that's exactly what they did. And what happened? It went away."

Because he believes Interscope followed up their lack of public support for Knight's plight with a private campaign to strip him of his premier talent, the conspiracy, as Knight has characterized it, becomes multi-layered. That Knight's violent business disposition worked to both he and his business affiliate's advantage, in that everyone reaped the financial profits those actions generated, worked to further justify its continued application.

To that end, the fact that anyone has attempted to characterize Knight's actions as singular, rather than as part of a collective campaign waged on the behalf of both Death Row Records and Interscope, sits in Suge's mind as the worst betrayal he has suffered since his incarceration: "As far as Jimmy Iovine and Ted Field, sure enough, there was a situation going on where…its like the oldest game in the world, you got a lot of racism, but I don't look at it like that, cause where I grew up in Compton, you didn't have time for racism…Everybody was just middle class or poor, so it wasn't about rich and it wasn't about poor, just people. But as time go on, people change, and you find serious racism when it come to business. And by me being ghetto, I was like naaah, you know, its not like that. But in my case it was like that. If, when Jimmy Iovine had looked at it and said 'Ok, Suge Knight got Death Row Records. He got the producer. He's got these artists.'…So when Interscope seen the whole game unfold, far as with Dre and Snoop, and then Pac, who was the biggest star of all of them, they seen the vision. They wanted it. And by me being a street guy I wasn't gonna let anyone come up to me and say 'I want your label, I want your groups, give it to me.' Because I was the only black guy to own his masters, his catalog. And they wasn't able to take it from me. But they was able to manipulate, and interfere with the contracts, and get my talent…And they was able to pull they scheme and they ideas off by me being in prison. Because there's two things that always safe to say about coming from the ghetto, either they gonna take the money from you, and if they can't take the money from you, they take you for the money. Only way to take you for the money is you dead or in prison. In my case, its prison. So its definitely a lot of situations that, its an eye opener, that people really gotta learn from, not my mistakes, but the way I was treated. Then if you look at it personally, before you judge me, you gotta look at the situation that was done to me." To this extent, Death Row's loyalists, be they artists or employees, are either BLOODS-affiliated or committed to Knight along the lines of a parallel mentality, and conditioned for lifelong loyalty. Ultimately then, those who have departed Knight in the wake of his incarceration are, by his rational, snitches or rats.

Chapter 4

The Death Row Family

Suge Knight has always considered Death Row a family, both as a concept, and as a reality. In describing his blueprint for Death Row's design, Knight clearly had an agenda in his desire to translate his own street background and credibility, and that of his neighborhood, into a commercial entity and reality, without skipping a beat or missing a detail with respect to its authenticity. In doing so, he expected his own work ethic to be that of his employees in their various facets, and held court with an iron hammer.

The difference between Knight and most of the African American entrepreneurs who had preceded him in trying to operate their own entertainment corporation with complete autonomy was that they had done so with a half step, always wearing a velvet glove in some fashion when dealing with their white corporate backers. Knight broke down this barrier literally when he forced Eric "Eazy E" Wright to release Dr. Dre from his slave-wage contract, which Jerry Heller (an old-era Caucasian music executive who had managed artists for years, principally in the rock arena) had negotiated. Heller and Wright's contracts with

Dr. Dre and West Coast hip hop pioneers N.W.A.'s other members had been dictated in the classic and unfortunate fashion that many of rock and soul's pioneering African American artists had been manipulated over the years, offering relatively modest advances against virtually no back-end royalty rate for commercial record sales. Additionally, all publishing rights were traditionally assigned to managers versus writers, in the case of N.W.A. that being Eric Wright and Jerry Heller, who had had no hand in crafting the sound that had made N.W.A. a sensation.

As a producer, Dr. Dre's role was unique because he was not only a performer, but also the creative center of Wright's record label, as Ruthless's house producer. In his four years with the label, Dr. Dre had produced 8 platinum albums, which by most industry standards would have made him a millionaire many times over based on stationary back-end percentages he was legally entitled to receive. Instead, Dre had been receiving a mere 2% of the royalties off sales his production work had generated. As a manager, Knight knew Dre socially, and upon consultation with Knight regarding his suspicions about payments potentially owed, and the obvious lack of lifestyle equality between himself and label owner Wright and manager Heller, Dr. Dre had felt a stinging betrayal.

The most unfortunate element to Dr. Dre's reality lay in the fact that he was legally committed to his arrangement with Ruthless for well over a decade to come. When Knight proposed an offer where, in exchange for Knight's obtaining Dr. Dre's seemingly impossible release from his artistic enslavement, Dre would partner with Knight in a record label both would own as equal partners, and in whose complete autonomy all creative and financial matters would reside, Dr. Dre had found his new home, and salvation from Wright and Heller.

In this union Knight had seeded the foundations of Death Row's family, and he subsequently made fast work of Dr. Dre's commitment to Ruthless in order to cement his own with Knight. As the Death Row family tree began to bud, with Knight clearly its principle caretaker, it did so much in the fashion of late Death Row artist Tupac Shakur's prose, A Rose that Grew from the Concrete, "Funny it seems, but by keeping its dreams, it learned to breathe fresh air. Long live the rose that grew from concrete when no one else ever cared", wherein Knight's philosophy was one which disbelieved in the institutionalized notion of adversity which American society had long sought to breed in its African American citizens. As a result, his approach was in many ways a happy medium between that of Martin Luther King and Malcom X's, wherein one favored non-violent protest to racial limitations over an extended period of time, best summarized in King's landmark 'I Have Dream' speech on the Washington DC Mall, while the other, that of X's, favored a more immediate physical retaliation to institutionalized racism.

Knight's method sought to center on a vision, and achieve it not by pretending racism didn't exist in the framework of the white-controlled recording industry, rather by entering into his negotiations absent the notion that racism would play any role in his deal, idealizing King's concept of a equal playing field, while applying Malcom X's approach of violent rebuttle to anyone who attempted to assign the notion of restriction or control over Death Row's potential for growth, principally by owning a part of its destiny. Ted Levine and Jimmy Iovine agreed to Knight's terms, and as a result, Death Row's urban roots quickly branched out into Beverly Hills' suburban ones with the distribution deal Knight secured with Interscope Records.

Adversity seemed alien to Knight in light of his steel confidence and ready application of physical threat or violence to convey the impact of that resolve. Knight did not view success as a competition that had room for a second place price, and in seizing his prize, he enlisted a team of players who were equally as hungry, and willing to do whatever was necessary to make Death Row what it became soon thereafter: "To have a vision, and believe in something, you gonna work hard at it. When I had my vision with the music business, my whole motive was to work hard and be the best at it. So I treated it like we was a football team. My background is athletics, far as being athletic, and being on a football team. So I looked at it like, well, (Death Row's) gonna be like a training camp. Having the artists, having the producers, having the writers, having everybody together. Where they eat together, and damn near sleep together, and they work together. And the chemistry's gonna sound better because the album's gonna be much fuller. Instead of an artist talking about me, me, me, me, me, its gonna be about a variety of different things going on." The result of Knight's blueprint was Dr. Dre's landmark *The Chronic*, completed in the latter half of 1991, and released in November of that year. Its impact would change the face of hip hop permanently, and chart much of operating course for independent hip hop labels in the latter 1990s.

Not only did Death Row's deal dispel the age-old notion of white-owned corporate control over African American-run businesses, but did so with a no-holds-barred approach that had only been witnessed in song and on video prior to Death Row's incorporation. Knight brought an authenticity to his business dealings in the label's early days that could not be denied, and as a result, Death Row emerged with a distribution deal through Interscope in which Knight and Dr. Dre maintained complete ownership of their master catalogue. *The Chronic*, in its commercial definition, referred to a grade of marijuana leaf that was considered an instant classic among those who smoked it, requiring only a single hit to reach a buzz.

A similar metaphor applied to the success of the album *The Chronic*, in that it only took one listen before rap fans nationwide were hooked, thus making Death Row's first release an instant classic, in line, metaphorically, with the effect of its title. Beyond its impact with record buyers however, *The Chronic* represented a personal achievement for Knight and his label family that not only validated his vision as a reality, but proved that the formula that Knight had fought to assemble was actually a successful mix when listened to. This only fueled Knight's already expanding ego, complimented by Death Row's growing viability as a hit making label. As one artist, Warren G, Dr. Dre's brother, who worked on *The Chronic*, commented a mere two years following its release, the record was representative of a family effort, helmed by Dr. Dre's creative and Knight's commercial visions, and realized in a community atmosphere that Death Row would readily display in its videos and press interviews as the record took off.

Death Row Records' reality as a hip hop powerhouse would not explode, however, until the release in 1993 of Snoop Dogg's *DoggyStyle*, which established Knight's label as the premier independent hip hop label in the country. There is no doubt that *DoggyStyle's* initial sales figures were helped tremendously by the fact that the same week Snoop Dogg turned himself in and was arraigned on first-degree murder charges for his alleged role as the driver in a gang-style drive-by shooting. While he was released on $1 million dollars bail, and heavily restricted in his movements by the trial judge's order that Snoop remain under house arrest, reporting home by no later than 10 at night, he didn't need to be in any more visible a position for Death Row's notoriety to grow by volumes— in record sales, out of stereo wolfers, and in the media as the press fed feverishly off of the gossip that Death Row's urban legend was churning out.

Behind the scenes, Suge Knight navigated Death Row's expanding aura of invincibility largely by steering around questions regarding he and his roster's open affiliation with violence as a problem solver, while hardly denying its presence. In an October, 1995 interview in *Vibe Magazine* with journalist Kevin Powell, Knight responded in kind to questions about his violent business disposition: "Powell: 'What about the methods you used to get (Andre Harrell) to renegotiate those contracts?' Knight: 'Its like this, was you there?' Powell: 'Nah.' Knight:; Then there's nothing to talk about.'"

The ironic brilliance to Knight's answer was that there was, in fact, plenty to talk about, and that he refused to respond only invited further speculation, directing Powell, or who-ever the media representative happened to be, to write in a very open-ended vein on the subject. In most cases, Knight seemed prone to only discuss the periphery of the violence sewn in Death Row's internal fabric: "We called it Death Row 'cause most everybody had been involved with the law…A majority of our people was parolees or incarcer-ated." In other words, Death Row's camp were OG's (orig-inal gangsters) going into the hip hop game, even if the label was still in its infancy in terms of industry longevity.

It was his ghetto experience that equipped Knight with the survival instincts to manage the mayhem that would follow with the release of Snoop Dogg's debut solo LP. Where other labels might have faltered under the pressure, Knight seemed only to thrive, implying he had more of a hold on the whirlwind than it could have ever had on him. That left only rabid hip hop fans to get caught up in the hustle that Death Row's reality-based sound was laying down on the streets: "Ghetto politics teaches you how to win and be real hungry. I never been one who wanted to work with nobody. 'Cause if a motherfucker get you a pay-check—listen to how that sound, paycheck, like they paying you to stay in check. Can't nobody keep me in check."

In many ways, the ordeal of Snoop Dogg's murder trial was Suge Knight's first real test as a CEO. In the same time, he had the challenge of managing both the meteoric rise of Snoop's star and the Murder charge that threatened to shoot it right out of the sky, before Death Row had any real chance to shine through it. On the outset of the release of *Doggy Style*, it was clear that the record had the potential to change the face of hip hop permanently.

Dr. Dre publicly stated his desire to outdo the success of his own debut album, *The Chronic*, which had served to intro-duce Snoop Dogg to the hip hop world, with the release of Snoop's solo LP. As Snoop would later recall in his autobi-ography, "When some writer asked him why it was taking so long to get my album out, Dre was quoted as saying that the tracks he was doing for me were 'the future of funk…I never heard of a perfect hip hop album…but I'd like to make one.'" While it was Dre's job to creatively hone Snoop's debut to become what popular hip hop jargon referred to as *tha shit*, Suge's job was to swat away all the flies looking to collect on the overnight sensation Snoop had become. This had begun months earlier when Suge had moved Snoop out of his gang-ridden Long Beach neighborhood to a more neutral territory of Los Angeles, a suburb appropriately dubbed Palms. Perhaps the move was targeted more at keeping Snoop on turf neutral to both the Crips (of whom he was a member) and the Bloods than at taking him completely out of the hood altogether, as the neighborhood of Palms was still located next to one of the worst housing projects in Los Angeles, Nickerson Gardens.

The only unique trait of this territory, and perhaps the reason why Knight had picked it given his intimate knowledge of the gangland turf in South Central Los Angeles, was that the gangs that ran in Nickerson Gardens were largely considered neutral to both the Crips and Bloods. In the eyes of Death Row, keeping Snoop away from both gangs likely served to limit the amount of trouble that could come his way while he worked day and night to finish Doggy Style. In the event that would ultimately serve to threaten the stability of Death Row's very foundation with Snoop's murder indictment, the neighborhood gang member he was accused, along with his body guard, of murdering, was part of a gang called the By Yerself Hustlers, because, as Snoop recalled, "they'd never been able to get hooked up with either the Crips or Bloods and were working on an indie tip."

While Snoop's neighborhood remained seemingly neutral of gang distractions, the same cannot be said for the making of *DoggyStyle*, which did not proceeded completely free of gang-related conflict. The most interesting aspect of the gang-affiliated undertone to the recording of Snoop's LP, and even his affiliation with Death Row, was the fact that Suge Knight's camp and Snoop's camp were on opposite sides of the street;with Knight's Blood affiliation, and Snoop's with the Crips. One would assume that Knight would be at least professional enough in the long run to put it aside in the interest of business and finishing what would be Death Row's first superstar release, but the meanwhile proved the opposite was true, as the recording sessions were filled with the type of drama that seemed unavoidable in the Death Row camp.

As the one seemingly independent variable Knight was not able to control, allowing gang culture to exist as prevalently as it did at Death Row ultimately served only to jeopardize the label's chances at legitimacy as the type of powerhouse Knight had envisioned. As Snoop recalled during the making of his solo LP, there was no way to avoid the gang-related drama: "(Suge) had Blood affiliations, and more often than not, the crew that would come down with him to the studio were some hardcore Blood bangers. To say that the situation created some tensions with the Crips that were our friends is to put it mildly. Sometimes we'd have to call a halt to the recording session because a fight had broken out in the booth, with Suge in the middle getting everyone worked up and taking sides, one against the other."

Regardless of the latter, the timing of Snoop's murder indictment and that of the release of his debut LP couldn't have been more of a perfectly accidental opportunity for Knight, and seize on it he did. As Snoop himself remarked following his arrest, which occurred the morning following his appearance as a presenter at the MTV Music Awards, Knight proved himself a true born leader in the way he delegated the aftermath: "I've got to hand it to Suge Knight. He was on the case from the jump, taking charge of the situation and coming at it from every angle he could think of, up to and including legality, publicity, and security." In this light, Knight's role as Death Row's CEO ultimately served to even out the loose-cannon elements of Death Row's culture that were so prevalent during the recording of *DoggyStyle*, as everything that followed its release had to play out as tightly the beats Dre had produced for the album, leaving little room for any excess drama. Knight had his hands full enough, and it is this factor that may have ultimately spared his label an early demise. When Snoop Dogg was launched into the stratosphere with his solo album's release, so too was Death Row, particularly Knight as he had the dual role of record CEO and legal manager.

In one of his shrewdest moves as an A&R man, Knight used Snoop's murder charge to publicly raise Death Row's reputation as the only truly authentic representation of the gangland experience, which at the time was the single most appealing factor to the masses of white record buyers who were eating up over 68% of hip hop sales nationally. By releasing Snoop's debut album the same week as he turned himself in on a murder charge, the synergy, though in reality accidental, of the two fed so perfectly off one another that to most record buying eyes it seemed all the more natural.

As the promotional campaign began for *DoggyStyle*, Knight only fed the fire by filling Snoop's videos with gang-friendly images and landscapes, highlighted by gang signs, colors, and images of his artists' packing firearms while engaging in confrontational behavior with rival gang members. MTV ate it up, playing Snoop's singles in heavier rotation than any other hip hop artist they featured. The Hip Hop press was equally as enthralled, featuring Snoop and Dre on the covers of *The Source*, *Rolling*

Stone, Vibe, and *Rap Pages* among others. Editorials in major newspapers like *The New York Times* and *The Washington Post* speculated on the effects that Death Row's gangland reality would ultimately have on the teenage masses who bought millions of Snoop's albums weekly, hinging the outcome of the latter question largely on that of his murder trial, which was still over two years off. As Snoop would remark in hindsight, "I had what you'd call 'instant credibility', and Suge and his team at Death Row used it for everything they could."

While the record buying public waited, they bided their time celebrating Snoop's arrival as the first authentic gang-affiliated rap superstar, remaining largely neutral to a judgment one way or the other about his guilt or innocence, as it was ultimately irrelevant in the face of his celebrity. Knight had on his hands a true superstar, much like Don King with Mike Tyson following his release from prison, Knight fed Snoop to an audience who was incapable of deciphering Snoop from Rambo in terms of their bottom line hunger for entertainment that was just real enough to provide an escape from their sleepy suburban existence. Dually, to the Urban audience Snoop catered to, he was a hero because even if he was guilty, largely for the same reason O.J. Simpson would later be, because he was one of the few black men capable of a white man's justice.

The bottom line for Knight and Death Row was that Snoop's album was celebrated by the public, revered by critics, and within the Hip Hop community, Death Row was quickly establishing itself as rap's most dominant trendsetter, and it was the label's authenticity that singularly distinguished it from competitors. As Knight would later recall about the height of Snoop's solo debut, "what made those records so important was, everyone was really living the life back then...Today's gangsta hip hop isn't real if it doesn't follow the guidelines we set at Death Row."

Those guidelines were set on a single principle of blurring the lines just enough to draw the record buying public into Death Row's gangster-friendly concept without scaring them away. Snoop himself confirmed the latter, explaining the correlation between Death Row's gang-friendly image and the desire by millions of suburban record buyers to be a part of that culture as one in which being down with Death Row "was a mark of genuine gangsta status that money couldn't buy. That logo on a CD was as good a guarantee for a chart-topper as you could get in the music business."

That guarantee came via a lot of hustle on Knight's end to capitalize on the drama surrounding Snoop's murder trial in as many ways as could be maneuvered, the result of which was 4 million records moved in just under six months. The public end of this campaign may have seemed natural, but behind the scenes it was a well-oiled machine that moved in the tradition of many hit records—without regard for the long-term effect on the artist. Though Snoop did get a 5,000 square foot home in the plush suburb of Claremont, California (purchased in his name against the advice of Knight, who wanted the house put in his wife Sharitha's, who was also acting as Snoop's manager, name), and a pricey legal defense (which ultimately cost Knight upward of $5 million), he was given little say by Knight concerning the manner in which the controversy the murder trial was marketed in conjunction with the promotion of Snoop's solo record.

The campaign culminated with the release of a Death Row soundtrack for an 18-minute movie starring Snoop and aptly titled "Murder was the Case". On the album's cover, Snoop is featured along with the chilling caption "In Beloved Memory of Calvin Broadus 1971–1994". The album was an instant success, following its predecessor to a debut at the top of the Billboard album charts, catering to both the hungry rap fans and the media who increasingly focused on Death Row as the gatekeeper to a new era of reality rap that could not be second-guessed. From Snoop's point of view, Suge took things too far in his marketing of the murder charge before the trial had even occurred, but he said nothing publicly about it at the time, unwilling as most everyone was to challenge Knight's authority: "I got the feeling that Suge had taken the whole publicity angle one step too far by trying to hook my situation into another opportunity to move some product."

The success of Snoop's debut album provides an interesting insight into the allegations that Suge Knight funneled much of the label's profits back into the Compton drug trade, in part, it has been argued, to repay investment debts incurred during the recording of Dr. Dre's *The Chronic*. The Death Row debut had a total price tag of between $250,000 and $750,000 depending on who you believe, not counting other label start up costs, which included an extravagant number of groupies who drained on Death Row's bankroll. As Snoop recalled upon visiting Dr. Dre's crib early on in Death Row's infancy, "When we showed up (at Dre's Crib), it seemed like there'd been a twenty-four hour a day party going on up there for the last couple of months, with homies and fine bitches just draped all over the leather furniture...like Dre was the daddy and all these homeboys and girls was his little children, holding out their hands for the goodies he could give out." The bottom line in accounting for all the expenses was that Knight had a lot of them to juggle. While it has been a media and lawsuit hobby to speculate on where Suge got his start-up capital, each alleged source has had a competitive share of drama attached. There is of course the proceeds from Vanilla Ice's publishing, which Suge controlled, as well as a $10 million start-up investment from Interscope Records, and the alleged investment on the part of Michael Harris to the tune of $1.5 million.

Harris's allegation is flimsy, and the best evidence of that to date has been the Justice Department's investigation into the aforementioned allegations regarding Knight and his drug ties to the Bloods enterprise, which failed to ever turn up enough to warrant a formal indictment. The aforementioned investigation, when it was first announced, caused a flurry of speculation in the media, and worry among Death Row's inner-camp as to what would be uncovered. Knight at the very least was guilty of creative accounting, irrefutable by the fact that every one of the label's artists eventually left Death Row with some kind of financial straits due to mismanagement on Suge's part.

Whether he was guilty of that mismanagement because he owed the money to individuals even more intimidating than he, is harder to buy when one considers the fact that most of the allegations against Death Row have to date remained just that—alleged: "The Government went through every detail of my background. And anybody that know me or knew me, any artists, every last one of them will tell you that we didn't start off rich. We didn't start off with...millions (of) dollars." No matter the angle one chooses to look at it, Suge Knight had a lot of debt to repay following the release of *The Chronic*, whether it was to corporate CEOs, or to ghetto-based drug dealers, it was not until the success of Snoop Dogg's solo album that Death Row began to throw its money around in the media like it was expendable. Even Knight himself has recalled Death Row's early days as meager ones, trying to play down the notion that money was flowing from the jump because of illegal investments, and push the image of Death Row as a regular business with a lot of bills, just like any other start up: "If we has any money from anyone else, we wouldn't have been going through the hard times we went through. People at PopEye's felt so sorry for us that the girls would give us a extra piece of chicken or a free roll to try to fill us up. The thing about it is, even if you ask Interscope, any time we did our deal, they had to give us our money immediately. It's not like we had money."

Snoop has backed up Knight's assertion, recalling Death Row's early days following the release and success of Dr. Dre's *The Chronic* LP as thin ones in terms of label artist pocket padding. Snoop, more than anyone, had grand expectations about the payday that might accompany his album's release. Another example of all that, for Death Row, was riding on *Doggy Style* being the success that it ultimately was: "you'd think that with the run we'd had with *The Chronic*, everyone involved would have enough juice to never worry again. But that wasn't the way it came down. While I can't tell you exactly what happened to all the proceeds from that album, I do know that none of us niggers were getting rich off it."

When Snoop's album did turn out to be a smash, Suge handled his business with everyone, reinforcing his better side as keeper of the Death Row family. He bought artists who hadn't yet released, or in some cases, even recorded their albums, houses and cars. As one Death Row employee, Doug Young recalled, the first week numbers on Snoop's debut LP, scanning 800,000 copies, was the first time that Suge really started spreading money around: "I didn't make a lot of money doing this Dre shit...But the Snoop shit? Everything came home...I made a gang of money... Definitely when this Snoop thing hit...That was raining Christmas. All good for everybody."

Some have argued that the spending splurges on Knight's part were designed to distract attention from his creative accounting, in turn allowing him to divert the monies he is alleged to have stolen from artist accounts to continually fund the elicit activities he was alleged to have been involved with. Publicly, in interview after interview, backed up by journalist's visits to artists' houses, or rides in their newly purchased luxury automobiles, Suge spread Death Row's image as a family that took care of its own around in the press as readily as he did luxury among his artist stable. The latter was clearly deliberate, but not in Suge's eyes toward any sinister end, but to further bolster his claim that Death Row was out to not only make superstars, but also take care of them as no label had before. One happy family, as he liked it to be referred to: "My mission is helping young black talent see their dreams happen... That's my ultimate purpose in this business, so fuck any-body who can't understand or deal with that."

It would be another two years before Knight's true inten-tions with respect to his artists' interests would be called into question. In the meanwhile, it was Death Row's lavish spending and gangster preeminence that attracted the attention of the hip hop artist that would come to mark Knight and Death Row's greatest commercial height, and ultimately reveal its lowest moments.

"Out on Bail, Fresh out of Jail, California dreamin'
Famous because we program
Worldwide let 'em recognize from Long Beach to Rosecrans
Its West Side, so you know the 'Row will bow down to No Man"

Tupac Shakur, 1995, *California Love*
Death Row Records

Suge Knight and Tupac Shakur attending one of Death Row Records' many community charity functions in Suge's home town of Compton, California.
AP photo

Chapter 5

The Sound and the Fury

Suge Knight and Tupac Shakur vs. the World

By December, 1995, Death Row Records' popularity had expanded enough to have become the coolest clique in hip hop's new school. Snoop's murder trial would soon end in a high profile acquittal, bolstering Death Row's dapper image, and in October of that year, Suge Knight had made international headlines and a $1.4 million dollar investment in what would become Death Row's greatest asset yet. In Tupac Shakur, Suge Knight found his musical soul mate, and the potential for a pinnacle position in Hip Hop that superceded even the controversy surrounding Snoop's murder indictment that had worked to propel *Doggy Style's* debut sales into the record books.

"Suge" Knight and two Death Row family members at the 1st Source Awards, 1995   *Photo by Walik Goshorn*

Death Row co-owner, Producer and Artist, Dr. Dre; Producer Sam Sneed, and DJ Quik in Compton making hits, 1995.   *Photo by Walik Goshorn*

Puff Daddy, and Biggie Smalls praying backstage before a concert at Madison Square Garden, early 1996.   Photo by Walik Goshorn

Kurupt (The Dogg Pound) producers Sam Sneed, Dr. Dre, DAZ (The Dogg Pound), 1995.   Photo by Walik Goshorn

CEO and founder of Death Row Records, "Suge" Knight, making his famous East Coast/West Coast speech at the 1st Source Awards with producer Danny Boy.

Photo by Walik Goshorn

CEO and founder of Bad Boy Entertainment, Puff Daddy, "Shakin' His Ass," at the 1st Source Awards show where the East Coast/ West Coast Rap Wars began, 1995.   Photo by Walik Goshorn

*Death Row Records greatest, Snoop Dogg and
Dr. Dre with Kurupt.   Photo by Walik Goshorn*

*Tupac, "All Eyez on Me," took Death Row to another level.
Poet, rapper, musician, philosopher, gangsta, nothin before
or afta like Tupac.   Photo by Walik Goshorn*

Shakur's kind of profile was unique in two principle ways. First, he was an established, multi-platinum rap and film star whose viability among the record buying public had been sampled by Knight when Shakur had worked with Death Row two years prior on the *Above the Rim* sound-track, which Shakur starred in, and which Death Row released. Though he was signed to Interscope and had a number-1 album, multi-platinum album, *Me Against the World*, still sitting high on the Billboard Charts, Shakur had been imprisoned since November, 1994 for a sex-abuse conviction, and was vulnerable. Second, and more impor-tantly, Shakur was Hip Hop's preeminent expert in land-ing himself directly in the eye of controversy's whirlwind. He was an on-screen natural, as had been proven in his cin-ematic work, and the media loved him. Where Snoop had learned to be a superstar in front of the camera, Shakur had the experience under his belt to act the part at the drop of any given drama. More importantly, he was seen by the mainstream as an icon, something that Death Row had yet to achieve with any of its artist roster. Tupac knew how to turn any controversy to his advantage, and in this way, Knight and he were perfect bedfellows.

In the months that followed Tupac's release from prison, he and Knight would be inseparable, and Tupac would raise Death Row's profile to a level of commercial success that took most labels ten or twenty years to earn. Knight had done it in just four, priming his pump with Dre and Snoop. With Tupac, it was time to blow up. Shakur led the pack by publicly praising Death Row for freeing him, and in the same breath, condemning Bad Boy for trying to end rise to the top, making them appear as natural rivals. Shakur announced his intentions in a interview (with *Vibe Magazine* journalist and friend, Kevin Powell) shortly after his release from prison, proclaiming " I promised...Suge,

I'm gonna make Death Row the biggest label in the whole world. I'm gonna make it bigger than Snoop even made it. Not stepping on Snoop's toes; he did a lot of work...(He and) Dre made Death Row what it is today. I'm gonna take it to the next level." One of the principle ways Knight and Shakur chose to fuel Death Row's album sales in 1996 was to capitalize on the media-created East Coast/West Coast feud that had erupted when Shakur was the victim of a robbery in October, 1994, in which he was robbed of $40,000 in jewelry, and shot five times. He publicly blamed New York-based Bad Boy records CEO Sean Puffy Combs and Notorious B.I.G. for the attack, and took out his anger in the media by waging an all out war on East Coast hip hop, as a style.

While Shakur played the antagonist on the Coastal front, Knight remained neutral to everyone but Bad Boy exclusively, targeting Combs as a weakling bordering on the feminine, and as an enterpriser looking to make himself a star on the backs of his artists. Suge had made his first public taunting at Combs a few months earlier, in August, 1995, at the Source Awards, when, while presenting an award, Knight announced to the audience, which contained a number of Bad Boy artists, "If you don't want the owner of your label doing backup vocals on your albums, shakin' his ass in your videos or on your tours, come to Death Row." From that night forth, on it was.

The media picked up on the conflict almost immediately, and erupted it into an all-out rivalry that was brewing steadily as Shakur served his term in prison. On the surface, neither Knight or Combs went out of their way to publicly confirm that a rivalry existed. For Knight, it was different principally in two ways.

First, he knew that Shakur had problems with Notorious B.I.G. over the robbery, and by generifying the conflict he took away from the heat that the specific rivalry between the nation's two fastest rising stars could draw. On that level, Knight left much of the trash talking about Biggie Smalls to imprisoned Tupac, who he very much viewed as a boiling pot waiting to overflow.

Second, Knight had a personal vendetta against Combs over the shooting death of his friend outside a record release party in Atlanta in which members of Bad Boy's entourage were implicated. When asked by reporters whether the beef, in fact, existed between the two camps, Knight's answers were never definitive one way or another, rather just vague enough to leave the door open for media speculation. He broke it down to basics that would have, in any other instance, seemed almost too simple to reach a mass audience. In this case, because the one man Knight targeted was also CEO of New York's pre-eminent rap label, the impact potential was much more volatile. In a sense, Knight was building something in the conflict between the two coasts that would explode upon his bailing Shakur out of prison. However, early on, his temperament was chillingly passive toward Combs and company. The principle reason for this position was because for Knight and company, the conflict would prove to be more real, and ultimately deadly, than the media could ever dream of contriving.

Asked by one interviewer whether Knight felt there was a beef between the two camps, Knight responded with a demeaning dismissal: "For what? I'm a man...I don't have no rivalry with no person in the industry...who's not a threat to me." Quietly, Knight was busy eliminating that threat, principally by working out the details of Shakur's bail and signing exclusively to Death Row, and as rumor had it, putting a contract out on Comb's head. As Combs would later respond, frustratingly to a reporter, "I heard there was a contract out on my life…I'm ready for them to leave me alone, man." But the battle had not yet even begun. In the three months that would follow Shakur's release from prison in November of 1995, Knight and company would quietly set the stages for what would, arguably, be the most explosive year in hip hop; making Knight, Shakur, and Death Row Records legendary in more ways than they could have wished. In the meanwhile, Knight left the question of an East Coast West Coast beef largely in the hands of media speculation, and focused on rallying his fiercest troop yet.

If the media chose to classify it as a Coastal dispute, Knight was content to let it be as such. It was clear to any objective eye that the journalistic community was intent on spinning it as a mass confrontation; simply because more papers got sold that way. Snoop Dogg agreed with the latter assessment, commenting that " Ask me and I'll tell you—East Coast, West Coast; Death Row and Bad Boy; Biggy Smalls and Suge Knight—most of what you hear about all those rivalries is shit the media makes up and splashes all over their newspapers and their time slots and their glossy magazine covers to make more money."

Still, Shakur's release from prison and signing to Death Row was celebrated as a victory for the West Coast the day Shakur set foot out of his cell. He immediately drew the battle lines in his first interviews with the hip hop media, singling Suge Knight and Death Row out as his only ally during his imprisonment, implying that the East Coast hip hop community that Shakur had been affiliated with in the months preceding   imprisonment had not only been behind his shooting, but also had abandoned him while he was incarcerated: "When I was in jail, Suge was the only one who used to see me. Nigga used to fly a private plane, all the way to New York, and spend time with me. He got his lawyer to look into all my cases. Suge supported me; whatever I needed. When I got out of jail, he had a private plane for me, a limo, five police officers for security. I said 'I need a house for my moms'; I got a house for my moms." As an added touch, a month later, he implied on camera during a video shoot, Suge by his side, that he had slept with Notorious B.I.G.'s wife, Faith Evans, who had done some backing vocal work on Shakur's seminal Death Row release, *All Eyes on Me*. All of Shakur's press for the release of his comeback album, recorded in 3 short weeks as raps first double LP to debut at # 1, was themed around the rivalry between Death Row and Bad Boy, which the media then would amplify into a beef which encompassed both coasts in their respective entireties. The public quickly caught on, and Shakur was on fire. Soon, the conflict was greater than the two camps, and it became a stylistic conflict in terms of which coast could produce the hottest product and sell the most records. Death Row clearly had a lead in the race with Shakur as their hip hop jockey.

Asked by one journalist to describe the title of his Death Row debut, *All Eyes on Me*, conceptually, Shakur set the tone and pace for what would be Death Row's momentum for the next ten months, eliminating all competitors, and generating over $80 million in sales off of Shakur's releases alone: "This comes from someone who just spent 11 and a half months in a maximum-security jail, got shot five times, and was wrongly convicted for a crime he didn't commit. This is not from a normal person."

Indeed. Shakur was Hip Hop's most sensational figure, and one of its most openly vulnerable. He had the ear of the entire hip hop community, and in the wake of his recent series of tragedies, their collectively sympathy and intrigue: "I learned...on the floor at Times Square (where he was shot 5 times in a robbery)...(that) I don't have any friends, I have family. You're either my all the way family or just somebody on the outside." More importantly, by embracing Knight as his father-figure while the nation embraced Tupac's rebirth as an icon, Death Row served as an unlikely catalyst for connecting Tupac with an entire new wave of fans, and for achieving a level of celebrity that, in his peek, was only appropriate.

Death Row's single greatest benefit, aside from the tens of millions of dollars that the label took in monthly off of Shakur's album sales, was that the label took on a new identity of its own. While violence was still an ever-present element of the label's culture, Death Row's presence now spoke for the West Coast, unified in a way that went against the grain of even Knight's age-old gang affiliation. Rather than focusing on gang rivalry, Death Row was finally at the point where it was at the center of a much larger beef that had national implications for the direction hip hop would ultimately head. Suge's battle plan for dealing with Bad Boy, who had now seen the numbers that the rivalry pulled for them in terms of record sales, readily engaged Shakur in his verbal war of words, both in print, and on record.

Unifying fronts between himself and Death Row, Shakur adopted a demeaning line of rhetoric that favored Knight's, casting Bad Boy in the role of the weakling: "My homeboy Suge gave me the best advice that I could ever get from anybody. When people ask him if he's beefing with Bad Boy and with Puffy, he says it's like me going to the playground to pick on little kids...They can't look at themselves cause they know the prodigal son has returned. I'm alive...and I'm going to...crush your empire. And that's what it's time for." And that was it. After that, it was on, and the battle was Death Row's to lose.

To add to the pressure which consumed Knight's life at this point, Snoop's murder trial was also concluding, and its outcome would either severely cripple Death Row or enhance its aura of invincibility. Suge took it all in his typically intimidating stride, expanding Death Row's assets and enterprises to the point where the bases were clearly loaded. As one reporter summarized the latter in a January, 1995 *Vibe Magazine* profile of the label, "this is an especially hectic time for Knight and Death Row, whose 'keeping it real' mentality has the industry all shook up." Part of what made Shakur's, and in this time, Death Row's presence so intriguing was the inherent lack of stability one felt in their collective midst. Everything had moved so fast for Knight and his camp that no one knew when it would slow down, but felt inevitably the label's beast-like momentum would have to be tamed by something.

With Snoop's fate pending in a murder trial that was in its own right a miniature version of what O.J. Simpson's had been, and Shakur's freedom contingent on a successful appeal, Death Row's fate was very much up in the air, though the label continued to rise skyward. Tupac's role in the latter equation was particularly affecting as he openly discussed the possibility of his death as though it were something imminent. The fact that he had narrowly escaped it once before made his dialogue that much more chilling. Snoop once described what he termed as Tupac's knowledge that he was fated to die young: "By the time I started running hard with 'Pac, you could almost see in his face the knowledge he had that death was closing in. A kind of haunted look would come up in his eyes when he thought no one else was looking, a sadness that didn't have a name and was gone as soon as someone called him back into the here and now." Tupac clearly lived life for the moment, which in a way contrasted him from Knight, who had long-term plans for Death Row that he was slowly implementing. By March, 1995, a month following the release and instant smash success of Tupac's *All Eyes on Me*, Snoop's verdict came down as a Not Guilty on all counts in the state's indictment. Suge Knight took the opportunity to discuss Death Row's plans for the future, including an immediate renaming of his label to "The New and Untouchable Death Row Records".

In addition to the release of near-future projects by Tupac, Snoop, and Dr. Dre, Knight also had a number of social commitments in mind which would add to the legacy he had already established in his hometown of Compton of charitable giving to his community. At a press conference following Snoop's acquittal, Knight spoke to the press about his plans for a Death Row-sponsored vocational school that would train ex-convicts in different trades, and continuation of a service that would chauffer family members from impoverished inner-city neighborhoods to prisons where their loved ones were serving time when the family members would not have otherwise been able to afford such trips.

Tupac shared Knight's belief in giving back to his community, and sought in interview after interview to outline his intentions to accomplish as much as he felt he could on that front before fate took him in what he felt was his destined direction: "There's a program called 'Celebrity Youth

League' with Me, Hammer, Suge, and all these sports figures are each going to sponsor a youth group all year in
football, baseball and basketball. We sponsor our team,
buy the uniforms, hire the coach and start our own little
league...We (are) also planning...to do a big concert with
me and (Death Row's artists) to raise money to have a
center in North Central where we can have the 'at risk' kids
come to a spot that that can call home—where they can get
guidance, tutoring, love, nurturing...but instead of it just
being a program with me and Tyson like I had planned...
Now I'm doing it with Death Row."

Charitable commitments aside, the most important
achievement feat Suge Knight had accomplished for his
organization during this period was the fact that with the
acquittal of Snoop Dogg and the signing of Shakur, Knight
had positioned himself to the point where he could succeed commercially without the presence of co-owner Dr.
Dre. Dre, who had established Death Row's commercial
credibility, and had remained vital to their first three years
of multi-platinum releases, producing his own solo album
and Snoop's debut, as well as supervising the production
on the label's two soundtracks, and mixing the Dogg
Pound's double platinum debut.

As Death Row had become more commercially viable, Dr.
Dre had reportedly developed two beefs with Knight; the
first being over the creative direction the label was head-
ing, with Dre desiring to broaden Death Row's pallet to
include more R&B releases, while Knight clearly preferred
hard core hip hop, exemplified principally in the way he
had prioritized the label's releases, pushing back the R&B
releases Dre had been working on, notably including that
of longtime girlfriend and mother of his child, Michelle'.
The other, and more important, disagreement existing

between Dre and Suge was over money, as Dre had alleg-edly grown suspicious of Knight's management of Dre's accounts. As Snoop recalled the latter conflict, " Sooner or later Suge's policies were going to come back to bite him in the ass, and the later became sooner when Dr. Dre started moaning about his profit participation in the Death Row money machine. "What made Dr. Dre's position look more legitimate than anything Knight could muster up in refut-ing it was the way in which Dre left Death Row—with nothing. In addition to giving up any claim on the master recordings he had produced, he also gave up any claims on Death Row's future earnings: "I just wanted to start over clean…where whether I fail or succeed, it is on me".

The fallout from Dre's departure from Death Row was felt more throughout the industry than internally. Knight moved on according to plan, doing a cover story with *The Source* where he trashed Dre's reputation, while Tupac trashed Dre on record and in his own interviews. When Death Row lost Dr. Dre, they clearly had lost their integrity in the eyes of many industry insiders, but no one would dare to call Knight on that fact.

At that point, Death Row had clearly achieved a status that paralleled that of modern day mobster John Gotti, who the media had dubbed "The Dapper Don" because of the number of legal acquittals he had racked up, and the sub-sequent aura of invincibility that had gone to his head. Col-lectively, Death Row's camp began to give off the same impression. Snoop's follow-up to *Doggy Style*, aptly titled *The Doggfather*, included lines like "Murder was the case that I beat". Tupac, in one of his last interviews before the night that ended his, and in many ways, Death Row's life, compared himself to the equivalent of a 'Black Jesus Christ', proclaiming that "I got shot five times and I got crucified in the media, and I walked through with the thorns on, and I had shit thrown on me, and I had the word thief at the top; I told that nigga, 'I'll be back for you. Trust me, it's not supposed to be going down, I'll will be back.' I'm not saying I'm Jesus, but I'm saying we go through that type of things every day. We don't part the Red Sea, but we walk through the 'hood without getting shot."

Tupac was certainly entitled to believe anything he desired about his destiny, and while he didn't walk on the water without getting himself wet, he was resilient in his determination to walk through whatever battle engulfed him with his flame raised as high as he could hold it. He was a true soldier in that light, and he made Death Row part of that war, but it could be argued that he was truly more prepared to accept the consequences of his actions than Knight, or anyone within Death Row's organization, ever were.

Tupac's journey was one in which he was prepared ahead of time for the end, seeming to keep it always in sight, and in this way, he was able to proceed with a much clearer headed direction than Knight, who thought he was untouchable. Tupac reaffirmed the latter assertion in one of the last interviews he did while he was alive: "God blesses those that hustle…I believe that everything you do bad comes back to you. So everything that I do that's bad, I'm going to suffer for it. But in my heart, I believe what I'm doing in my heart is right. So I feel like I'm going to heaven." Suge Knight took a largely opposite perspective on the fate of Death Row in an interview he gave to MTV shortly following the death of Tupac Shakur, refuting the notion that Death Row could suffer any great loss in the absence of their biggest star: "We gonna do things we've been doing, and sell our records…I'm not gonna sit down nowhere. I'm gonna walk the pattern, talk the same talk…"

Perhaps Knight felt this invulnerable because he sat with the security and knowledge that, while Tupac was alive, he had recorded over 150 songs for Death Row, whereby Knight would have material to release for many years to come. The body of work that Tupac Shakur accumulated during the nine months that he was out of prison and signed to Death Row is impressive by any standard, and surpassed what most recording artists rack up in their entire career. In addition to his recording catalog of 150 plus completed tracks, Tupac also starred in two movies, and shot nine music videos, including one he directed. More importantly through, the amount of finished product he racked up serves as the best evidence to support the notion that Tupac knew his time was short. In a poem he wrote discussing his death, aptly titled "In the Event of My Demise," Tupac remarks on the latter realization in the context of what he hoped he would have accomplished: "I will die Before My Time, Because I feel the shadow's Depth, so much I wanted 2 accomplish, before I reached my Death."

Whether Knight pushed him toward that end because he wanted to make as much revenue off of Tupac while he was still around, or succeed as an artist in every available outlet he could, or possibly for reasons more sinister, Knight was clearly inspired by Tupac's drive, and readily credits Tupac for pushing Death Row to the heights it achieved while Tupac was alive and recording for the label: "Tupac loved Death Row. Tupac loved me. I loved him. I mean, Tupac took Death Row to the next level. I mean, we worked hard, we laid the foundation down, Snoop took the baton and he ran with it. He did a great job with it, but when Tupac got the baton, not only did he win the race, he finished so fast he able to sit back and drink some thug passion in, and come up with another play."

More than the professional achievements, it seems in reflection that Knight found his soul mate in Tupac. Though the two were inseparable for a number of reasons, while Tupac was alive for the last 9 months of his life, they clearly had a shared affinity for each other's drive, and vision with respect to the role Knight wanted Death Row to play in terms of the direction Tupac sought to take hip hop.

People will speculate for years about what Knight's true intentions were in his friendship with Tupac, but his death clearly affected Knight as a human being, no matter the fact that he may have been conflicted in his management of Tupac's finances. He clearly had an affection for Tupac that superceded business, and came from the mouth of a man who watched his best friend die: "(The last thing 'Pac said to me was) that he loved me. You know, he was going... he was gettin' there. I'm like, 'Pac, you're gonna be the last one left.' But we talked this out. We talked it. He said, 'No, I'm straight. I love you, homey. I'm gonna be straight.' I love you too. That's where he was."

The latter serves, at least to some degree, to refute the allegation that some have lodged at Knight that he in fact was responsible for Tupac's murder. No where is this more evident than in Knight's comments to the Judge who revoked his parole a short time after the murder. When talking about the impact of the year 1996, Death Row's biggest, Knight referred to the loss of Tupac as one of the most difficult tragedies he had ever had to face. Tupac shared this sentiment in one of his last interviews, paralleling he and Knight's solidarity to that of a military front, seeking to wipe out the competition completely: "Everything I don't have, he's got, and everything he don't got, I got. Together, I think we can only be stopped by each other. We want, not oppression, but total domination. I'm banging for the

Wesside. It's in my heart. When I be throwing up the W it ain't for California, it's for war. We still all separate tribes, and I know what tribe I'm in. I'm a soldier. I'll always be true to those who are true to me."

Nevertheless, the demise of Tupac Shakur marked the beginning of the end of an era for Death Row Records. The fallout from Tupac's death would rock the world, and would shake hip hop to its very foundations. While many have speculated that Tupac knew it was coming, Death Row's biggest deficit in its aftermath would be the fact that Knight had no idea of the latter. In the days preceding the fateful day of September 7, Tupac and Death Row Records would display their greatest aura of arrogance yet, likening themselves in interviews to a Mafia organization, wherein Suge was like a Godfather, and Tupac a Capo. Ironically, Tupac made most vocal comments on the subject on the set of his final film, ironically titled "Gang Related," at a time when he was clearly caught up in tidal wave Death Row was riding, and in a moment when he had no idea, nor care it seemed, of when that wave might crash: "Suge is the boss of Death Row, the Don, you understand? But I'm the under boss, the Capo. That's my job, to do what's best for all of Death Row."

If Tupac had succeeded in making Death Row feel invulnerable, then the label's behavior, chiefly that of Knight's, in the aftermath of Tupac's murder, was appropriate. They, as a collective unit, were desensitized to the potential impacts such a tragedy could, and indeed would, ultimately have, and as a result, did very little to adjust in its wake other than turn to Knight for direction. The problem was that Knight was nowhere to be found.

Suge Knight holding Tupac Shakur back from News cameras on the night of his fatal shooting, just following the completion of the Tyson/Sheldon fight in the lobby of the MGM Grand Hotel.   *AP photo*

Suge Knight and Tupac Shakur leaving for Club 662, just minutes before Tupac was gunned down along the Las Vegas Strip. This is the last known photo of Tupac Shakur alive.

AP photo

Chapter 6

9-7-96 R.I.P.

On September 7, 1996, Tupac Shakur's life ended. So too did a part of Suge Knights'. The night's tragedy marked the beginning of the end of an era. While the work Tupac Shakur had completed during his eight months with Death Row would serve as the label's lifeline in the years to come, Shakur's demise would, in a more immediate setting, mean that of Death Row's position at the pinnacle of hip hop's elite. Shakur had foretold his own fate many times over in the course of his career, particularly during the last year of his life, and in a way, by doing so he had already prepared his fans for the seemingly eminent possibility.

The one it took by surprise over and above anyone else was Suge himself. Though in the aftermath of the murder, he would maintain a rigidly passive exterior, in truth he had lost his most kindred spirit in the death of Tupac. This was most evident in an interview conducted with MTV shortly following Tupac's death, when Suge was asked about how the shooting had affected him in a general respect, his focus was clearly centered on the loss of Tupac.

In his answers, Suge revealed in a raw, emotional expression the love that had governed their kinship, principally in discussing how they had both shown more concern for one another's welfare over their own in the minutes immediately following the shooting: "I feel like this: I feel that the last word is always God, but Pac saved my life. He's my...Pac saved my life. I got shot in the head—got grazed some other places...Before, I was tryin' to get him to the hospital—didn't make me realize that I was shot. Because usually, when you get shot in the head, the first thing the person do is panic. You know, BAM! I'm shot in the head! I'm about to die! And once you do that, you can't drive nowhere. My whole thing was Pac—he was shot. I'm like, 'You're shot! Let me get you to the hospital.' I'm driving, telling him I'm gonna get him to the hospital, kicked back, Pac looked at me and said, 'You know what? You need a doctor more than me. You the one shot in your head.' And we laughed the whole time finding our way to the hospital. That's the conversation we had."

That week the world wept with Suge Knight. The affect of Tupac's death was sweeping, touching almost every (facet) of pop culture in one form or another. In many ways, Tupac Shakur had become hip hop's John Lennon; its soul. As the personification of a culture's collective angst and hope, Tupac hadn't broken down walls, he had walked straight through them. Adversity was a transparency in the presence of his indomitable spirit and universally appealing charisma. When ten months earlier Tupac seemed to have reached his peak of Pop stardom, sitting in prison with a number one album and a declaration that "Thug life is dead," he was in truth at the very beginning of his journey toward the superstardom that signing with Death Row Records would bring him.

Tupac Shakur's launch into the top of the pop stratosphere was as seemingly eminent as his coming demise, which he wove as a central element into his music and message—that time was short and therein precious. By the time word spread that he had signed with Suge Knight and Death Row Records and was on his way back into the recording studio to finish what would become his best selling album to date, the eponymous *All Eyes on Me*, which was recorded in 3 weeks, and quickly became hip hop's first double album to debut at number one on the Billboard Pop Chart and sell five million copies in two months, millions of fans were frothing at the collective bit.

When Knight set Tupac free, the reaction from fans was much like the crowd at a racing track when the buzzer first sounds the horses out of the gate, a crazy wind of anticipation and almost simultaneous release. Tupac was hip hop's thoroughbred, recording an astonishing 150 songs in the eight months between his release from prison and death in Las Vegas. The entire time, Knight was his shadow, and in turn, Shakur in many ways Knight's light. They played off one other brilliantly, as kindred spirits, and as an unstoppable business force, eclipsing the success of any other hip hop artist, or label for that matter, in the history of the genre.

Such that, in the immediate aftermath of Shakur's death, Knight had made an eerie peace with the fact that Shakur was gone, shown principally through his confidence when asked about Death Row's future without their marquee artist. Possibly this was because Suge quietly knew that Death Row owned enough completed Shakur material to release albums well into the next century, and therein had already planted the cornerstone of its legacy. Closer to heart, however, Knight seemed to have shared in Tupac's acceptance that his demise was as inevitable as his rise, that the two went hand in hand. As a result, Suge was not in a position at the time of Shakur's death where its reality was something he was still processing, as the rest of the world was. Rather, he had already accepted it, and made his own peace with its being fated. In his recollection of the final moments he and Tupac shared, Knight clearly reflected this peace, which was clearly rooted in a mutual respect and admiration that only the closest of friends can share: "(Tupac's last words were) that he loved me. You know, he was going...he was gettin' there. I'm like, 'Pac, you're gonna be the last one left.' But we talked this out. We talked it. He said, 'No, I'm straight. I love you, homey. I'm gonna be straight.' 'I love you too.' That's where he was."

Many of those watching Knight, whether as a part of their own agendas or because they only chose to understand Death Row's close knit psychology superficially, missed the affinity between Knight and Shakur, choosing instead to judge the relationship based on Knight's refusal to coop- erate with the police in their quest to solve the mystery of the shooter. Some speculated that Knight's silence was rooted in his loyalty to the laws of the gangland he had been raised in, which forbade cooperation with the police in solving homicides, even if the victim was part of the gang members own family. As Knight and Shakur appeared as close as brothers, many couldn't comprehend the notion that Knight would remain quiet in the face of the whirlwind desire on the part of the press and hungry hip hop fans to solve the mystery of Shakur's murder. Knight was content to let them make the noise.

Outside of discussing his love for Tupac, Suge seemed to have little else to say, because for him personally there was no need. He was quietly mourning, but in the same time took comfort in the knowledge he was at one with the peace he and Tupac had reached with one another through their collective accomplishment. To that end, Knight didn't talk, to the police, or much to the media, because he didn't have too: "Tupac loved me. I loved him. " Suge, by remaining silent, was in truth remaining loyal to his best friend's wish to leave the earth in true peace, free of any lingering question that he was hip hop's true prophet, or as Tupac himself had put it in an interview conducted shortly before his death, he had become the Black Jesus: "I got shot five times and I got crucified in the media, And I walked through with the thorns on, and I had shit thrown on me, and I had the word thief at the top; I told that nigga, "I'll be back for you. Trust me, it's not supposed to be going down, I'll will be back." I'm not saying I'm Jesus, but I'm saying we go through that type of things every day. We don't part the Red Sea, but we walk through the 'hood without getting shot. We don't turn water to wine, but we turn dope fiends and dope heads into productive citizens of society. We turn words into money-what greater gift can there be? So I believe God blesses us, I believe God blesses those that hustle. Those that use their minds and those that overall are righteous. I believe that everything you do bad comes back to you. So everything that I do that's bad, I'm going to suffer for it. But in my heart, I believe what I'm doing in my heart is right. So I feel like I'm going to heaven."

Unfortunately, back on earth, the media and the police were hungry for someone to blame, and Suge, through his silence, gave off the impression to the shallow mind of the viewing public that he had something dark to hide. By this point, Suge's reputation had grown in notoriety enough to raise even the theory that he personally had been behind the murder as rumors surfaced shortly after the murder that Tupac had planned to leave the label. Despite the ludicracy of the notion that Knight would have himself risked being shot in the head, which he in fact had been, to cover up suspicion, the notion worked to insult Suge more than it did to hurt him. As he responded to one media pundit who questioned Knight about the suggestion that Tupac had planned to jump ship, Knight refuted the notion based on his firm belief in the mutual love and brotherhood that he and Shakur had found in one another, and that had in turn worked to elevate Death Row to an unspeakable height by what were, at the time, the conventional standards for hip hop commercial success: "You don't take a person like Tupac, who, if you listen to every song on *All Eyez On Me*, every song on "Machiavelli," every time he do an interview, what's the first thing he say? Death Row. Tupac loved Death Row...I mean, Tupac took Death Row to the next level. I mean, we worked hard, we laid the foundation down, Snoop took the baton and he ran with it. And he did a great job with it. But Tupac got the baton, not only did he win the race, he finished so fast he able to sit back and drink some thug passion in, and come up with another play. If you'd asked Tupac that question that was he planning on leaving Death Row, he definitely would have cussed you out."

Nevertheless, the seed of suggestion had already been planted, and soon its reverberation throughout the hip hop community was felt by more ambitious entities who were looking for a way to shut Death Row down. Whether Knight would have avoided the incarceration that followed a short two months later, in November, of 1996, by cooperating with the authorities on the outset of his arrest, is doubtful. With Shakur gone, Death Row Records was already beginning to lose its balance. Dr. Dre had been gone by this point for over a year, and Snoop's follow-up to his Dre-produced smash debut was not anticipated with the same excitement that had fueled earlier Death Row releases. The label still released the post-humunous Shakur title *Makievelli: Don Killamunati—The Seven Day Theory*, which featured an eerie portrait of a crucified Tupac on the cover, and the soundtrack for Shakur's last movie, "Gang Related," as well as Snoop's *The Dogg Father* to platinum, Billboard # 1 debuts, but Tupac's murder clearly marked the beginning of the end for Death Row Records, and made Knight law enforcement's number one target.

As the media swell began to focus on Knight as the sole witness to Shakur's murder, his movements began to become the hunt of every tabloid news reporter within a 1000 square miles of the mention of Suge's name. Of course, the papers focused in on Knight's criminal history, and in doing so, in conjunction with their intense spotlight on his every step, started the ball's true unraveling. First, reports of a video tape from the MGM Grand security cameras emerged which purported to show Shakur embroiled in a beat down with his Death Row entourage of a rival gang member, Orlando Anderson, who the Las Vegas police had now begun to speculate was responsible for murdering Tupac in retaliation to the beating.

As the tape made its way onto the nightly news, replayed thousands of times over in the course of the week immediately following his demise, it became quickly apparent that Knight too had been party to the beat down. If the events captured on the MGM video tape had truly been the catalyst for Shakur's violent demise, then Death Row's live for the moment philosophy had finally caught up with its architects, as the incident ultimately cost Shakur his life, and Knight his freedom. Once the world had been made aware of the video, so too were the Las Vegas, and subsequently, the Los Angeles Police Department. Knight's silence during this period, not only about the details of what he witnessed in the course of the shooting, but also with respect to offering any interpretation of the events captured on video the night of September 7, left it largely up to the authorities and media to draw their own conclusions. In doing so, Knight became more the villain, and the District Attorney's office in turn began to consider Knight for the role of election year whipping boy. Perhaps Suge's silence concerning an explanation of the video-tape beat down was designed, at least in part, to avoid giving the media the satisfaction of exploiting the death of Tupac further than they already had? Or possibly he had no justifiable explanation for his entourage's actions that evening? Whatever his reasoning, he would not formally address the content of the video until almost a half year later when Suge sat before Judge Czugeler at his politically-charged probation revocation hearing.

In the meanwhile, Afeni Shakur filed a lawsuit against Death Row Records alleging that Knight had cheated her son out of tens of millions of dollars in royalties, and the fallout from Tupac's death rocked hip hop to its collective foundation. Speculation ruled over explanation because there, in truth, was very little in the way of one. Tupac Shakur's murder had been largely senseless. To some, it was a tragic example of life imitating art. To others, it was inevitable given the fast lane Tupac lived his life in. Knight was blamed largely for the latter, encouraging Tupac down the decadently glamorous path that the Death Row family traveled. Now as the world looked for someone to blame, Suge quickly transformed in image from Tupac's keeper to his deceiver. His motives became suspect, and suddenly, Death Row fell from an impenetrable position to one of fragile vulnerability. Without Knight's micromanaging presence, Death Row faced almost an inevitable period of decline.

The question of when that slide would begin was answered in November of 1996, when, at the height of media speculation regarding the cause behind Tupac's death, and in Knight's most vulnerable moment, he was ordered incarcerated for several minor probation violations that would have otherwise gone unnoticed had the media not been scrupulously tracking his movements: "Tuesday, October 22, Suge wore brown three-piece pinstripe suit swaggered by news cameras in front of the courthouse...Inside, Judge Ouderkirk said he had repeatedly given Suge the benefit of the doubt. To let him walk free would be an embarrassment. Looking down from the bench, he read a long list of Suge's failures to make appointments for drug tests and court appearances."

The true catalyst for Knight's arrest had been the MGM video tape. The Los Angeles District Attorney's office were fixated on Knight's role in the September 7th brawl as their key to ending a dry spell in celebrity convictions. With a tough re-election campaign ahead of him, DA Gil Garcetti targeted Knight, picking up on, and through the arrest, fueling the media characterizations of Knight as an authentically violent presence in hip hop, as evinced, they argued, by his involvement in the Shakur murder, even though he was technically a victim. Suge Knight was now a monster who had to be kept off the streets for the sake of public safety. Though the media had celebrated Knight's notoriety when Tupac was alive, they now painted Suge as a menace who had coerced favorable press only through threats of violence. One conveniently anonymous report even suggested that Knight had held a journalist above a fish tank of piranhas when he disliked the reporter's questions in the course of an interview. Now that Knight was off the street, people were free to take shots at him without fear of Suge's iron fist striking back. The results of this free-for-all not only proved to be a tragic miscarriage of justice and gross violation of Knight's civil rights, but also forced Knight to deal with his demons. Therein, the principle upside rested in the fact that the experience, specifically his initial incarceration while awaiting his sentence for the probation violations, inspired in Suge an introspection that the public had not witnessed before.

In his address to Judge Czugeler, Knight wore his heart very much on sleeve in pleading for his freedom, sharing with the court, and in affect the world, not only how the events of the past year had affected him personally, but what he truly thought of the allegations that had been lodged against him. In a strange turn of events, Knight appeared to have come full circle within himself, and had to some degree, as a result, seemed to have already accepted his fate as a sacrificial lamb to the political wolves. Though in later years he would express an equal bitterness toward those who had turned their backs on him, Knight at the time of his revocation hearing seemed a mix of frustrated but adjusted to the reality of what had encompassed him: "I'm not here to try and sugarcoat my life and say I've been the most perfect guy in the world. But...I've learned a lot from being incarcerated. I've gotten closer to God and I've read the Bible inside out. I've learned that my role in the community is important as far as kids...I do a lot of good in the community and I don't do it for publicity or fame. The stuff I've done has come from my heart...When I walk through this court room, I see the DA say everybody hates me; I'm this bad guy; I'm this monster and I don't see it...I believe in the community, cause its all I've ever had. I've seen mayors, even the president, give speeches and say they gonna give back to the community, that they'll hire people from the community. And we never see it. When I was growing up, it never happened. So when, thanks to

God, I was able to make a little money and do these things, I done them. But instead of someone giving me applause, they slander my name…I've been in a cage for five months, where they feed me when they want to feed me, and they give me water when they feel I should have water. And I was this close to dead, 'cause I (got shot) in the head. Being in prison has made me realize that I definitely don't want to do my life behind bars. But if its more positive for the community by me being incarcerated, I'm willing to sacrifice. I'm willing to give my life for a friend or for kids…I been through a lot this year. I lost my best friend. A lot of people don't realize how it is to lose a friend. I always wanted a little brother, and now he's not here…But when the media gets it, it turns around that I left him for dead, I left him with zero, and that I'm the monster. Whether its my competition or prosecution, they made me look like Frankenstein…As far as the situation with the fight…Your honor, I was breaking up the fight. I knew I was on probation. I put my freedom and my life on the line. And I feel like if I wouldn't have stopped that fight—I'm not saying the same person who came and shot us later was these type of people, but if they was—instead of me getting shot in the head and (Tupac) dead, it could have been thirty people dead in Vegas at the MGM. And in the end, your honor, when everybody say 'it was a kick', it wasn't a kick. I admit that I was breaking up the fight, and I admit I was frustrated; but at the same time, its not a nine year kick…I'm not gonna waste any more of the court's time, but I just thought it was important that I get this off my chest, and address the court the way I feel."

In a round about way the latter may have worked to soften the public's perception of Knight as a monster without remorse or compassion, and for any of those watching who were willing to look past Knight's criminal record, revealed a man who had carried the weight of several worlds on his shoulders almost singularly, as the president of a multi-million record company, as father figure to a community of fatherless young, African American males whom Knight supported through legitimate jobs in the Death Row organization, to the community he invested millions of dollars worth of Death Row's proceeds back into.

At the heart of his hearing, Suge Knight was revealed to be simply an extremely driven and intelligent male, born into poverty, who had worked extraordinarily hard to climb out of the ghetto, and who had built the first legitimately and wholly black-owned record label. At the height of his success, rather than turning his back on his community, Knight had committed his heart and soul to revitalizing it. While all the ugly allegations regarding Knight's business tactics were made public at his revocation hearing, so too were the plethora of kind hearted deeds he had done for his community, that had irrefutably come from his heart. In the end, however, political pressure would govern the direction of the hearing, and Knight would ultimately, through a combination of perjured testimony, largely unsubstantiated allegation, and gross legal violations of his civil rights, face a nine year sentence of incarceration for contributing, on video tape, a single kick to a group altercation. Whether he was even breaking up the fight by involving himself in it still remains up to debate. Nevertheless, the DA had their fish caught in a net of lies and conjecture, and they were determined to reel him in, no matter what the cost for civil liberties.

Suge Knight's bullet-riddled BMW following the fatal shooting of Tupac Shakur.
AP photo

Suge Knight coming out of seclusion to visit Tupac Shakur in the Intensive Care
unit at Las Vegas's main hospital shortly before Shakur was taken off life support.
AP photo

Chapter 7

"Have Gun" Unravels

'Ronin Ro' and the Campaign to Make Suge Knight...a Monster"

O, f all the allegations that have been lodged at Knight and shots taken behind his back over the course of his four year incarceration, the most scathing is documented in the tabloid-esque "Have Gun Will Travel: The Spectacular Rise and Violent Fall of Death Row Records", a laughable vat of speculation and grossly irresponsible journalism, whose allegations are based largely on enterprising Knight opponents, random attention-seekers, and anonymous "industry" sources, all of whom could be considered about as credible as jail-house snitches. Most of those who do go on record in the book have a lawsuit of some kind pending against Knight and company, and the credibility of almost every accuser of Knight's can be called immediately into question based on their obvious biases against Death Row. In a jailhouse interview conducted in 1999, Knight himself provided the best description of the fictional campaign Ronin Ro's bastardpiece was clearly a part of, dubbing it part of "a conspiracy to make me a monster."

That campaign had actually begun two years earlier, at Knight's probation revocation hearing, when the prosecution team, lead by vindictive OJ Simpson District Attorney, William Hodgman, sought to paint Knight as Al Capone's evil twin, pulling out all the stops in what was clearly a one-sided hearing. In Ro's depiction of the hearing, he tries equally as hard to make Knight and his team look as guilty as possible. From irrelevant descriptions of Knight's lead attorney, David Kenner's "ill-fitted suit", to ridiculous suggestions that because Death Row artist Danny Boy, of whom Knight was legal guardian at the time, burst into tears when his caretaker was sentenced, the two were involved in some sort of a homosexual affair.

The inference on its own is absurd, but the evidence Ro cites to back up his claim is even more laughable, asserting that "after Danny Boy's outbursts in the courtroom, rumors surfaced that (Suge) and Danny were having a relationship." According to who?!!! Ro's sources for this allegations, like so many others in his fictional work, consist of a conveniently anonymous 'record label executive', so well spoken that, in his quoted passages which Ro's uses to try to back up this book's most ridiculous claim, this 'executive' rambles through an irrelevant, third-person dialog littered with 8th-grade jargon, claiming "then the person who told me was like 'Man, it looked like that type of shit, like…your woman would cry for you. Like, Oh Shit! You Kno'msaying? Now I'm wondering what the hell is going on?" So was any sensible, halfway intelligent reader. If the testimony offered at Knight's probation hearing had been littered with baseless trash in the vein of the latter individual talked, his case would have surely been dismissed, on the spot. Ro even becomes so desperate as to attack Death Row supporter MC Hammer's attire, calling unnecessary attention to what he rudely concluded "seemed to be (the rapper's) only suit…the threadbare gray one with the Nehru collar worn in every magazine photo session". (Who cares?) Ro adds an extra touch of bad taste by suggesting that Knight's attorneys, including Death Row Records chief counsel, David Kenner, were all working pro-bono at his probation revocation hearing. Again, the reader is forced to ask oneself where Ro is headed?

Beginning with Ro's unengaging narrative, and rambling writing style, which chugs along as slowly and unevenly as a nineteenth-century broken down boxcar train, the testimony of the hobos housed inside this fictional concoction ultimately amounts to nothing more than a tabloid transparency. Critics first hailed this book as meticulously researched, however all but a few have failed to point out the book's greatest single weakness, the credibility of its sources.

Offering largely heresay testimony about Knight's brutal management style and a host of unsubstantiated charges that range to include everything from drug-dealing to rape, Ro's work of fiction is told for the most part in the second and third hand, in which the book's so-called "eye-witness accounts" would never hold up under even a half-ass, public defender-sponsored cross examination. Taking, for example, the book's weak attempt at a suspenseful ending, which discusses a Justice Department investigation into allegations that Death Row operated as a drug front, based on the still-unsubstantiated charge by Michael Harris that his drug profits helped found the label. While Ro, with an arrogant air of certainty, states that "once the probe concludes, indictments will be handed down," none ultimately ever were. Knight himself addressed the allegations that Death Row was funded by drug funds by defusing the bomb-shell-that-never-was with simple logic, rebutting that "the government went through every detail of my background", referring to the federal probe.

One of the most disturbing problems with the allegations lodged against Knight in Ro's book are the glaring inconsistencies in both his research into the areas of Suge's own life, as well as those lives of the supporting hip hop characters he weaves sloppily into his fictional accounting. In example, after example, Ro takes completely unnecessary personal shots at Death Row-affiliated artists, notably including rapper and producer DJ Quik, who ultimately signed with East Coast-based Profile Records, at one point referring to the MC as "a frail Compton rapper who talked tough in interviews but wore his hair in an overblown perm to record a song."

In an even bolder example of (misstatement), wherein Ro is just wrong, he attempts for no apparent reason to discredit Dr. Dre as a genuine producer, though the multi-platinum genius has been honored with multiple trophies, including the prestigious Grammy Award for Producer of the Year, and platinum placks for his skill behind the mixing boards. Nevertheless, Ro again hacks at the trunk with his scissor-thin blade of credibility, citing a lawsuit friendly, failed music manager named Lamont Bloomfield as one of Ro's few on-record sources, who without any real basis with which to do so, concludes the "Dre's...not a real producer...As for playing instruments and everything people are hearing...Its everyone else, but Dre gets the credit for it."

The first rebuttal to Ro and Bloomfield's ludicrous claim can be found on the back of every Dr. Dre-produced record where there was a co-producer, such as Mel Man (in Dre's more recent work), Sam Sneed (on a few mid-90's tracks), and in his early days as N.W.A.'s mastermind, with DJ Yella. Conversely, on tracks where Dr. Dre was the sole producer, he is duly noted as such, including from the D.J. Yella-era, D.O.C.'s *No One Can Do It Better*, Dre's solo debut, *The Chronic*, Snoop Dogg's debut smash *DoggyStyle*, and more recently, selections from Eminem's debut solo LP, including hits like "Guilty Conscience" and "My Name Is...," as well as Snoop Dogg hits like "B-Please," and "Buck-Em." Bloomfield ends his chapter by concluding that "Dre knows how to manipulate nice guys".

Ro follows Bloomfield up with an poor and inadequate attempt of his own to discredit Dre's production skills by trying to tear down the brilliant remix of the hit Snoop Dogg single "Murder Was the Case," referring to the track as a "remix (with a) torpid drumbeat, drab heavy metal bass line, and fatuous pop keyboards" that, in Ro's opinion, "were dreadful". Because of Ro's Quincy Jones-level status as both a music producer and critic, he is surely qualified to insult a producer both hip hop and commercial musicians, industry veterans, and premier music critics have hailed as "the Phil Spector of rap". Ro in this same chapter, this time playing movie critic, refers to the Tupac Shakur movie Above the Rim, as a "lousy film about basketball and drug dealers." Over $50 million worth of people disagreed with Ro at the box office.

In another unnecessary and irrelevant instance, Ro takes a shot at his favorite target among the clan of Death Row rappers who did not go on record in his book against Knight, that being Danny Boy, Ro describes the R&B

crooner at one point as resembling "a scarecrow in baggy jeans" who followed Suge on stage at an awards show "trailing like a hound." That Ro would have to stoop as low as to insult an impoverished orphan who Suge adopted because the singer's grandmother was dying is just sad.

In yet another occurrence of gross inaccuracy, Ro, in describing Death Row's headquarters at the multi-million dollar recording facility, Can Am, referred to the studio as "a studio located in a tiny industrial park in the middle of nowhere". Ro's trash dump also happened to have been the cross-genre home in the past to multi-platinum acts including Motley Crue, and Bobby Brown. Ro even went as far in describing Death Row's set up within the studio as to compare Suge to drug dealer Tony Montana after Knight had a security system installed in the studio, sneering that "like...the Cuban drug dealer...Scarface, Suge had workmen install surveillance cameras over every inch of Can Am Studios... (trying) to watch everything in the building." Ro concludes his ridiculous rant of unfounded, and more importantly, unproven allegations by declaring that "at the label, Suge distributed...to his Blood henchman... his misogynist philosophy...that (like) Tony Montana... Suge felt real men should earn money first, then party with women." According to who?!!!

The aforementioned examples of repeated exaggerations and inconsistency pale, however, in comparison to Ro's attempts to establish a pattern of violence and brutality in Suge's approach and character. Ro time and again relies on the convenience of unidentified sources, bold enough to accuse Suge of every violation outlined in the California penal code but not man enough to do so on record. Highlights in his arsenal of bullshit are one instance in which Suge allegedly shot four people in front of a restaurant, wherein, according to Ro "legend had it that out front they had a gunfight and Suge wounded four people", with Ro conclusively ending the story with the bombshell that "no one knows if this ever happened". Exactly, no one knows! But that doesn't stop our author, who went on to claim that, according to 'someone close to him at the time', Knight became "Suge...the Don". According to Ro, Knight's tendency toward violence continued to expand out of control, to the point where Ro even goes as far to accuse Knight and his henchman of brutally beating down a woman, alleging that "even young black women were dragged into the room...(where) there'd be these two motherfuckers beating a woman up for doing something 'wrong'...They'd beat that bitch down!.Niggas done beat that bitch down!" Ro's alleged source was an 'insider' who remained, as usual, anonymous. It is disgusting that, without substantial support for his allegations, Ro would accuse Knight of ordering such crude and inhuman violations. This from a man who, sitting in a jail cell facing a nine year prison term, still found time to order holiday meals be disbursed to hundreds of single mothers.

Hardly objective, the most dangerous element of Ro's narrative is the fact that it has gone largely unchallenged by anyone in the mainstream media or music industry, not because of any legitimacy to its allegations, but because the book caters entirely to the one-sided impression of Knight as a malefactor. Ro completely dismisses Knight's long history of charitable giving as nothing more than sugar coating designed to act as a decoy to distract attention from his criminal enterprising. In affect, Ro succeeds at devoiding Knight of a human side, and denies him any dignity or opportunity to possess any of the genuine qualities he has clearly displayed as both a father and a community benefactor. Manipulating various quoted passages from past interviews, Ro seeks to make Suge sound arrogant and heartless. The latter occurs most notably in Ro's depiction of Knight's comments and actions during his probation hearing, wherein the confused author attempts to portray Knight's lawyers efforts to bring to the judge's attention Suge's charitable involvement in giving back to his community to counter the prosecutions claim that Knight used Death Row solely to advance his personal agenda of violence as something ulterior.

To that end, Ro paints Suge's interest in such an agenda as contrived and rehearsed, wherein "'Suge nodded like a churchgoer'...'Her testimony seemed to be an attempt to expunge Suge's bad reputation...(during which) Suge nodded in agreement'." The latter portrayal of Knight occurs most irresponsibly when Ro describes Knight's plea to Judge Czuleger, portraying Knight's tone as "a voice... (of) quiet menace". Why is Ro so determined to cast Knight as a monster? In a merciless smear campaign, Ro pursues Knight as though he holds some sort of personal vendetta, cutting him no slack as a human being. This, arguably, is the single biggest failure of Ro's campaign.

No one, even Suge, has denied that his past includes documented instances in which he resorted to violence. Knight himself attempted to explain that history in context to Judge Czuleger during his sentencing, beginning by addressing the prosecution's allegations of that he embodied a randomly violence-prone temperament, admitting that "I'm not here to sugar-coat my life and say I've been the most perfect guy in the world". As he tried to the put his criminal convictions, particularly those linked to acts of violence, in perspective, Suge made a very logical argument to the Judge, explaining that "in the past, when I was working security in the music business, a few times I had fights. Those were fights in my hands. I'm guilty for those fights, and I got punished for them." Knight's lawyers had supported the latter by pointing out that two of Knight's probations, both of which had resulted from confrontations to which Knight was party, had been successfully completed without incident. Knight, having offered some context in which to frame his history with violence, then tried to bring before the court his good-hearted, charitable side, possibly hoping one might work to at least, to some degree, outweigh the other in the court's final judgment of Knight, viewing him in a more genuine light than that of the media glare, which the prosecution clearly preferred he be seen in.

To that end, Knight explained in his most heart-felt plea that "I do a lot of good in the community and I don't do it for publicity or fame. The stuff I've done has come from the heart...I'm not trying to be a politician. I believe in the community because that's all I've ever had...So when, thanks to God, I was able to make a little money and do (charitable) things, I done them." Then, pointing at the prosecution, and tabloid media journalists like Ro, Knight made his truest remark of his entire plea, pointing out that "instead of someone giving me applause, they slander my name."

While the prosecution, along with Ro, had waged a one-sided campaign before Judge Czuleger to paint Knight as a violent and self-interested manipulator, Knight offered a compromise in which he not only would conform to a more model civil existence, which D.A. Hodgman had argued he was incapable of doing, but would also cease to allow certain elements of his label's product to exist which were among the most basic and fundamental elements to the formula for a successful rap album in the commercial medium Death Row sold in, offering that " I've made my own decision that any album I put out, the artist can never use the word 'nigger'." In an even more selfless moment, again wholly uncharacteristic of the image the prosecution team and Ro had put forth, Knight offered to put his own freedom at stake if it would ultimately serve a greater community good: "If it's more positive for the community by me being incarcerated, I'm willing to sacrifice."

Even Ro had dismissively run through Knight's charitable activities during his preliminary incarceration, citing among other directives that Knight had "instructed Death Row employees to prepare for their fourth annual Thanksgiving turkey giveaway. He wanted the birds distributed to the poor families that would appear at the Compton Fashion Centre parking lot the next morning." By doing so in the manner he chose to, Ro had without realizing it revealed a fundamental truth which served to largely contradict his thesis concerning Knight's evil-spiritedness. Ro even quoted a Compton Counsel Woman, Marcine Shaw, as praising the holiday effort, announcing that "even with…Mr. Knight's present inconveniences…this shows that (his) concerns are still with the community."

Why would someone who cared only about their own selfish interests, especially in a time when it would have been most natural and appropriate for he or she to focus exclusively on their own welfare, be so concerned with ensuring what had been a rich and well-documented history of community giving continued? In fact, Knight had begun his charitable campaign of giving back to the inner-city neighborhoods of Compton years before the hearing that day, and his actions to that end had been well documented in the media. In one profile of Knight, conducted in, 1995 ironically titled "HitMan" in referring to his golden touch as a platinum record breaker, *Vibe Magazine* journalist chronicled a lengthy list of well-documented community events Knight had sponsored. To fit his thesis, Ro often took Suge's acts of community giving and recklessly compared them to those of the most notorious gangsters of past 40 years, in one passage likening Knight to a mobster, who "like John Gotti with his Fourth of July cookouts and fireworks displays...continued to publicly promote the image of street-smart philanthropist."

In another passage, Ro randomly ties together Knight's rivalry with Sean Puffy Combs and his philanthropic giving within the same attempt of portray him as a gangster. What one has to do with the other is any reader's guess, aside from a weak reference to the East and West Coast rivalry, (which Knight denied time and again had anything to do with his beef with Combs), but Ro still drones senselessly on, remarking that "despite his verbal attacks on New York-based record label Bad Boy Records...Suge still found time to appease at the August 29, 1996 ceremony for A Place Called Home, a safe house for youths. At the ceremony...in South Central, he stood near Mayor Richard Riordan...(announcing plans) for...a benefit concert...(whose) proceeds...would go to a safe house, which offered alternative schooling for children, dance classes, and Gangster Anonymous, a counseling service modeled after the 12-step programs used by recovering addicts." (Sounds good! Where's the problem?)

Knight himself would address the contrast between the reality of his agenda, and that the prosecution and Ro had sought to contrive, arguing to the Judge that "whether its my competition or prosecution, they made me look like Frankenstein." Continuing, Knight then tried to stand up for himself, stating matter-of-factly that "I don't agree with all the things that (have been) brought against me...as far as my reputation."

In directly addressing his role in the fight that occurred on September 7 at the MGM Grand, Suge himself offered up the best analysis to date of what his role in the melee truly was, apart from the prosecutions or Ro's exaggerations. While he is clearly defensive, Knight in readily admitting his involvement puts the impact of his action in a rational perspective, absent of the dramatic extremes the prosecution tried to imply with what was in the end a single kick, arguing that "I was breaking up the fight. I knew I was on probation. I put my freedom and my life on the line...I admit I was breaking up the fight." In contrasting for the court what the extremity of his role would have been were he truly involved in a fight, as the prosecution had claimed, Knight illustrated where on the scale of impact his action truly would have measured out to a logical mind without an ulterior motive, pointing to the fact that "this guy wasn't harmed, wasn't anything broke on him. If you ask anybody that seen me fight, your honor, the first thing they'd tell you is...When I fight sir, I fight...But I've changed my life to get away from fighting...(and) it wasn't no nine-year kick." And in truth, he was right. What was captured the night of September 7 on the MGM security tape was nothing more than a single kick.

That single action was the foundation for the judge's decision to revoke Knight's probation, and ultimately for Knight's attorney's appeal. Though David Kenner's appeal would argue the latter point more eloquently to the California Court of Appeals, in truth the miscarriage of justice in Suge Knight's sentence was as simple at its core as Knight had stated before the judge. His action on the night of September 7 was not severe enough to warrant the court imposing a full nine-year sentence.

Kenner had attempted to compromise with the court, arguing that even if Knight's action warranted some punishment, the 375 days he had already served was more than an adequate term of incarceration. By Kenner's logic, the time that Knight had spent in jail was at best proportional, and at worst, already excessive: "These five months have been severe, shocking, draconian...It's not appropriate for there to be a state prison sentence of any sort." Still, Ro chose instead to ignore the logic in this argument, characterizing Kenner as just another of Suge's co-conspirators, at one point concluding that in "Kenner's eyes, the issue wasn't whether Suge violated probation by kicking Orlando Anderson."

Conveniently, Ro spared such characterizations for those Death Row employees who spoke on record against Suge, and in line with Ro's bloated and sensationalized thesis. As a journalist, Ro had a responsibility to consider all angles of Knight's story. However, as his work of fiction clearly displayed, Ro was no different in his bias toward Knight than any number of other enterprisers who sought to make money off of Suge, and Death Row's misfortune. In Ro's case, it was book sales. In the case of his interviewees, it came major idly in the form of pending lawsuits. Either way, the majority of those who spoke out on record in Ro's book had an interest in doing so against Knight—the principle reason why it is hard to find anyone among the book's 372 pages who had anything to say in Knight's favor. Ironically, out of Ro's book Suge gained one unusual ally in someone who had historically been an enemy of Death Row. As Ro had recklessly gone about making his case, he had painted Jerry Heller in the same slanderous light as he had Suge's supporters, which Heller was clearly not. Despite Knight and Heller's differences, the benefit of highlighting Ro's mistreatment of Heller in the book lies in principally in illustrating the lengths to which Ro would ultimately go to make Death Row and Knight fit into his convoluted thesis, despite the fact that both rarely did. After he filed libel suit for misrepresentations Ro made about Heller in his manuscript, Doubleday appealed and secured a demurrer in Los Angeles Superior Court which halted Heller's suit from going forth. In appealing, Heller argued, and the court agreed, that "the book...contained a false statement about Heller that was 'libelous per se' because it exposed Heller to contempt and had the tendency to injure him in his occupation, journalist Mike Diamonds reported."

Ro's use of no name Gang members clearly looking for attention as informational sources to substantiate his claims of Knight's criminal background is a particularly disturbing element of fiction. With the integrity of a wive's tale, Ro again and again relies on unsubstantiated accounts from alleged gang members to detail Knight's early days in Las Vegas as a drug-dealing football player, never allowing Knight the opportunity at any point in his life to simply be an African American male who worked hard scholastically and athletically to earn the opportunity to be a prospect for the NFL Draft that Suge ultimately became. Citing unnamed teammates to substantiate his claim that Knight was involved with drugs, Ro steps over the line early on, claiming through one alleged neighbor who conveniently remains unidentified that "he always had some guys that used to come up from Compton and...do some deals. I'm'a be honest with you: Suge made a lot of money...hustling, always making loot...Only a few people knew about him being in the drug game." Convenient.

In another disturbing instance of pure, unadulterated fabrication early in the book, Ro himself sets the stage by described Suge's formative years as a series of steps toward his development into the violent criminal that Ro claims he ultimately became. Offering no credible supporting evidence whatsoever, Ro enters into a rambling rampage about Suge's childhood, wherein he "played football… using any dirty trick he could get away with (to win)… (later) hiring himself out as a bodyguard…(beating) disorderly club goers to a bloody pulp; then…associating with drug dealers and in their presence beat people's faces with enough force to shatter bone; then, during nights on the town, he argued with bouncers and battered them to the point where their spleens were damaged and required multiple surgeries." From there, Ro launches into on a random and wild series of accusations that hold no water based on his sources, and work more to discredit Ro's argument before he has really had a chance to make it. His flavor of journalism leaves a sour taste in most sensible readers' mouths, and his hit-below-the-belt approach only makes him look that much more desperate. So to was the District Attorney's office.

Chapter 8

"It wasn't a Nine Year Kick!"

Following the high profile acquittals of both OJ Simpson, in October, 1994 on first degree double murder charges, and Death Row superstar Snoop Dogg in March, 1995 of first degree murder charges, Los Angeles District Attorney Gil Garcetti was looking for a fresh catch to fry in the tough re-election he faced that year, and Marion "Suge" Knight looked to be the perfect patsy. As Knight's lead attorney, David Kenner, would remark during the probation revocation hearing that would follow, the District Attorney's office was having its share of difficulty "convicting celebrities." Presiding Judge Czuleger, from the hearing's outset, demonstrated a clear preference toward the prosecution, at one point brushing aside Knight's attorneys to the point where David Kenner was forced to broach the issue, asking matter-of-factly "I'm boring you?" The Judge responded dismissively "It's my job to keep things moving along."

In doing so, Judge Czugeler made a number of rushed judgments that would later serve as the basis for the California Court of Appeals decision to overturn Knight's sentence; ordering a new hearing with a much broader array of sentencing options. Though the State Court of Appeals would ultimately have their order reversed by the California State Supreme Court, who would later reaffirm Judge Czugeler's initial sentence, the crux of what ultimately proved to be clear evidence that political pressure was applied to keep Suge Knight behind bars lays in the initial decision to the Court of Appeals.

In November, 1996 Suge Knight was sentenced to nine years in State Prison for participating in the assault on Orlando Anderson that was captured on the MGM security camera. The sentence was based on Knight's violation of several probations he was serving at the time, one stemming from a federal illegal firearm possession conviction (which ultimately resulted in a brief three month sentence in between June and August, 2001), and a more major violation of a 1995 no-contest plea that Knight had entered into with District Attorney Lawrence Longo for a 1992 assault on two aspiring producers who had mouthed off to Knight when instructed not to use a Death Row office phone. Under the terms of the latter agreement, according to Knight's appeal to the California Court of Appeals, the Judge stated that "Mr. Knight, essentially, will be placed on five years of formal probation...and the court will be suspending the high term of four years plus the five year high term enhancement, total of nine years on each count, and those counts will run concurrent...If he picks up a new felony of any kind, this case and his prior convictions in Nevada would make the new case a third strike case and he could get 25 to life."

While the concurrent nine year terms seemed clear in their definition at the time, the first Judge had left several doors open in the wording of his sentence which, by design or accident, none the less, provided more latitude in the options that the presiding Judge would ultimately have in passing sentence.

The first crucial point in the Judge's initial wording is the flexibility that was inherent in the deal's structure, standing in stark contrast to Knight's probation revocation hearing, where the Judge had ruled he had "no choice but to impose the original nine year sentence" as outlined in the plea agreement. In fact, according to the wording of the Judge's initial ruling, he had cautioned Knight that "when you plead to this particular case **the range** is going to be nine years state prison should you violate any of the terms and conditions of probation."

Clearly, the Judge had left the sentencing door open to a range of options up to nine year were Knight to violate his probation. Confusing matters even further, the initial trial Judge made conflicting statements as to whether he was in fact imposing the nine year sentence, or leaving the door opening to its imposition should probation be violated, remarking during the proceeding that "if he violates probation in this case…then he is going (to prison) if the court finds him in violation of probation and imposes sentence…Imposition of sentence is suspended. The defendant is placed on formal probation for a period of five years." This could have been deliberate to support the notion that there was a range of up to nine years available in the sentencing options that would be available to a court in judging Knight.

However, the Judge then contracted this flexibility in his closing remarks, stating that he had imposed sentence, where he had earlier stated that he was in fact suspending its imposition: "I have imposed sentence today and suspended it and placed the defendant on probation." At the revocation hearing, it clearly worked in the favor of Garcetti to ignore the fact that the trial Judge had in fact left the door open for a lesser sentence than the nine year maximum, and Judge Czugeler played right along, acting as though the option had never been available to him. To this end, he had stated he had "no choice" but to impose the nine year option, when in fact the Judge's initial ruling had left the door open to any number of options.

In the State Supreme Court's subsequent ruling overturning the lower Court of Appeals, the panel ruled that despite the fact that the Court of Appeals clearly felt that Judge Czugeler had more flexibility in his sentencing options than he had chosen to consider, based partially on the Judge's conflicting statements regarding his imposition of sentence, it was in fact Knight's fault that Czugeler had ignored the range of options because his attorneys had failed to clarify the flexibility in the initial hearing, ruling that "Knight's counsel did not object...or request correction or clarification. Consequently, we conclude that the trial judge imposed sentence and suspended its execution."

This ruling is clearly biased because of its illogical rigidry, and works to support the notion that the District Attorney's office had a clear end in mind with Knight's incarceration that reached beyond the immediate threshold of Knight's potential danger to greater society. Gil Garcetti was desperately looking for a victory, and the fact that Knight had been sentenced to a nine year prison term for possibly contributing a single blow to a fight speaks volumes to the lengths that Garcetti was willing to go, no matter how it clearly violated Knight's civil rights, to secure both his celebrity conviction and subsequent reelection. In simple terms, as Knight's lawyers would later argue to the State Court of Appeals, the trial Judge presiding over Knight's initial no-contest plea had deliberately left his wording vague because he felt there was room for a wider range of punishment options, and that "nine years" should not be the bar, but the extreme, or top end of available options. This does not negate the notion that Knight should have served some prison time for his involvement in the Orlando brawl, but the notion that it was worth nine years in prison clearly an exaggerated one, fluffed in part by political pressure from the District Attorneys reelection pains.

In recognizing that the imposition of the full nine-year sentence was extreme based on the severity of the action that had caused it, i.e. Knight's single kick in the Orlando beat down, the California State Court of Appeals in August, 1998 ordered a new hearing for Knight wherein they ruled that Judge Czugeler had not in fact been bound by the nine year sentence but had a much broader array of options from which to choose in sentencing Knight. The Court of Appeals, in ordering the new hearing, had also found fault with another, more fundamental, element of the initial plea bargain, wherein the District Attorney had agreed to reduce Knight's felony assault counts to misdemeanors upon successful completion of the five year probation term. This condition had not only been agreed to by the District Attorney but also by the presiding trial Judge, when it was impossible for either party to agree to as such an compromise was not permissible under California state law. Because both the District Attorney and Trial Judge had respectively agreed to this term, the California Court of Appeals later had found that "the plea bargain was invalid because the state promised to reduce his two felony counts to misdemeanors, which is not allowed under state law," overturning the nine year sentence and ordering a new hearing.

As the State Supreme Court pointed out in its own ruling, "the only circumstance under which 'the sentence automatically, upon initial sentencing, converts the felony to a misdemeanor' is where the court, at the time of conviction, exercises its discretion under section 17, subdivision (b) (1) to punish the offense as a misdemeanor instead of a felony...The assault convictions were not sentenced as misdemeanors 'upon initial sentencing' and therefore would still count as 'strikes' even if they were subsequently reduced to misdemeanors'." While this clarification should have worked to first reprimand the presiding Judge, the court chose instead to use it to punish Knight further, seeming to criticize his lawyers for pointing out the discrepancy as part of their appeal. The error was the courts, not Knight's. This fact is irrefutable. The Supreme Court had never disputed that. Nevertheless, they chose to ignore it as reason to find fault with Judge Czugeler's excessive sentencing.

The California Supreme Court would ultimately overturn the State Court of Appeal's reversal of Judge Czugeler's order, in a ruling that stands out as one of the most egregious displays of bias in favor of the government in the history of the violation of minority rights in our country's legal system. Beginning with their rejection of common sense arguments made by Knight's counsel to their willingness to allow the District Attorney's office grossly unjustified and unwarranted leeway in the mistakes they made in their dealings with Knight, the State Supreme Court clearly displayed the type of bias against Knight that could only have come as a result of outside pressures. Aside from the misrepresentations made by the District

Attorney with respect to his authority to promise Knight felonies could be reduced to misdemeanors according to the terms the two parties had initially agreed, (which any logical defendant would never have agreed to had they known such a compromise was illegal), and the deliberate latitude the Judge's ruling displayed regarding the "range" in Knight's sentencing in the case where a violation of probation occurred, one of the most clear examples of bias in this case comes with the Supreme Court's rejection of Knight's argument that because the terms of his initial plea bargain had been illegal, there is no way his deal could have been legally enforceable.

To that end, Knight's lawyers filed a petition for a *writ of corarn nobios* seeking to withdraw his plea, wherein the grounds of the petition consisted of the fact that "there was no mutual understanding as to the prosecution's end of the bargain—that upon completion of probation the assault convictions would be reduced to misdemeanors and not count as strikes under the three strikes law, and even if the prosecution did agree the convictions would be reduced to misdemeanors and not count a strikes, the prosecution's performance of this agreement was legally impossible." The Court's reasoning in rejecting Knight's lawyers on this point–that he had waited too long. This determination had initially been made by Judge Czugeler, who had ruled that Knight had failed to act within a reasonable time in seeking to set aside his plea, waiting until November, 1996 to withdraw it. (That's because he didn't know it was in fact illegal until the probation revocation hearing!) The Trial Court chose to pinpoint the initial entry of plea by Knight, in February, 1995, as the starting point for where Knight could have found fault with the terms of the plea and begun proceedings to withdraw it. That he had waited until his revocation hearing to call the terms into question was logical, given that Knight had no motivation to do so prior thereto. Once it became clear that the court intended to violate his probation based on a single kick (which under any other circumstance with any other defendant would have amounted to a C-grade misdemeanor simple assault, for which Knight would have paid a fine and been sentenced to an anger management class and possibly an unsupervised probationary term,) Knight's attorneys took appropriate action in exploring the legal ramifications of Knight's action as it related to the terms of his probation.

When Kenner and company discovered that the terms of Knight's probation had in fact been flawed, they sought to withdraw his plea. They could have not predicted such action might have been necessary until the biased nature of the hearing became clear. The Supreme Court in its ruling chose to manipulate the latter facts to sound off at Knight, rather than in the sensible harmony with logic and law that the Appellate Court had in overturning the illegal sentence: "Even assuming the plea bargain was based on a critical mistake of law, Knight has failed to establish a reasonable excuse for waiting more than two years to move to set aside his plea." In attempting to justify their denial, the Court seems to contradict itself by pointing out that "there is no time limit within which to file a petition for writ of coram nobis". They instead focus on the requirement of *due diligence*, wherein "a petitioner must show 'the facts upon which he relies were not known to him and could not in the exercise of due diligence have been discovered by him at any time substantially earlier than the time of his motion for writ." Wouldn't the fact that Longo had misrepresented to Knight his authority in agreeing to a reduced charge, which was the reason Knight had entered into his no contest plea in the first place, serve as grounds enough for Knight to qualify under the category within the definition of *due diligence* where he was operating under a false assumption put forth by the District Attorneys office? Furthermore, he would have had no cause to explore the possibility that this agreement was unlawful until it was clarified at the revocation hearing by the trial Judge. Judge Czugeler clearly ruled that Knight acted too late in contesting the plea because it suited the course he wanted the hearing to take, in collusion with a hungry District Attorney. The conspiracy would eventually reach as high as the State Supreme Court when they, without real justification given the aforementioned review of the circumstances surrounding Knight's timing in his writ filing, ruled that "the trial court acted well within its discretion in finding Knight failed to act with due diligence in seeking to withdraw his plea."

The California Supreme Court in its ruling on this point even went so far as to defend the conduct of District Attorney Lawrence Longo, who by this point had been dismissed from his job with the Prosecutor's office because of what had been determined to be substantially improper affiliations with Knight at the time of the no-contest plea, including the well-publicized signing of his daughter to a record deal, and the renting of Longo's Malibu beach house to Knight for $18,000 a month. This sort of ethically questionable connection clearly served to make Longo biased toward Knight, wherein he might feasibly bend over backwards to present Knight with a plea bargain that was ethically questionable, or even illegal, as it turned out to be. The fact that Knight may have enticed Longo to the aforementioned end is less relevant than the fact that Longo took a bite of that forbidden apple. In the legal arena, the fault clearly lays with the Prosecutor; who at that point had displayed a clear disregard for ethics in his approach to handling Knight's case, such that he was severely reprimanded by the California Bar Association for his misconduct. Nevertheless, the Supreme Court seemed to ignore what both the Bar Association and the District Attorney's office ultimately agreed was Longo's mishandling of the case, choosing instead to suggest that the plea agreement was somehow still viable, commenting that "leaving aside for the moment the issue of impossibility of performance, for the district attorney to deliberately breach a plea bargain entered into by a deputy would be 'a gross impropriety'...Furthermore, it is clear that...Longo had at least ostensible authority to enter into a plea bargain on behalf of...the District Attorney. Therefore, the plea bargain entered into between Knight and Longo and approved by the court was binding...even if Longo exceeded his actual authority when he entered into the agreement."

This sort of finding defies all logic. Clearly, it was Longo who had violated the law by leading Knight to believe he was capable of working the magic of reducing a felony to a misdemeanor when he must have known it was legally impossible. If not Longo, then certainly the trial judge? Nevertheless, Knight was ultimately faulted for being duped into this deceitful pact. Furthermore, the court penalized him for attempting to withdraw from the agreement once he realized it was legally unenforceable, even though they admitted in the same ruling that Longo had been the one in the wrong. If Longo had led Knight to believe that his plea was legally enforceable when Longo knew it in fact was not, how then would Knight be able to know he was entering into an illegal pact? Furthermore, how could one argue that Knight and the DA were on the same page when it turned out that the DA had misled Knight? Where the Court of Appeals had agreed with this logic, the Supreme Court nevertheless chose to ignore its truth, ruling simply and in clear bias that "we reject

Knight's contention his plea bargain should be set aside for lack of a 'meeting of the minds'."

One of the grossest and most disturbing violations committed by the Supreme Court in their ruling against Knight is found in their rejection of Knight's arguments toward why the order revoking his probation should be reversed. These arguments were based directly on the conduct of the Judge and District Attorney in the course of Knight's revocation hearing, included allowing a police officer to give perjured testimony, and permitting a Prosecutor to lie to the court.

In Suge's appeal, his attorney's pointed to four principle arguments as to why Judge Czugeler's order revoking his probation should have been reversed. The first and most negligent of these errors involved a the prosecutor's calling as a witness at Knight's revocation hearing a Las Vegas police detective who had been working the Tupac Shakur murder in the months prior to refute the testimony of Orlando Anderson, the victim in the MGM Grand video beat down, in defense of Suge Knight. Anderson had testified at the hearing that Knight had actually been trying to break up the fight as opposed to being an aggressor to the brawl. The prosecution contended that he had been coerced into testifying as such by Knight, and they called Las Vegas Detective Becker to refute Anderson's claim, as he had allegedly confided to Becker a month earlier that Knight had in fact attacked him. Detective Becker had purportedly been in Anderson's Lakewood neighborhood assisting local police in serving a search warrant, and had coincidently encountered Anderson, who at the time had been placed under arrest for an unrelated murder, sitting handcuffed in his driveway. As documented in Knight's appeal petition, "according to Becker, at the time he approached Anderson and questioned him about the fight in the Las Vegas hotel he viewed Anderson only as a victim of a battery and his purpose in speaking to Anderson was simply to find out what the fight had been about. He denied his purpose was to explore a possible relationship between the incident involving Knight, Shakur and Anderson and Shakur's subsequent murder. He also denied Anderson was a suspect in the shooting of Shakur." Unfortunately for Becker, one of the prosecution's principle witnesses against Knight at the hearing, on an affidavit filed in support of the search warrant, it was revealed that Detective Becker was in fact integrally involved in the Tupac murder investigation, in which Anderson was the Las Vegas police department's primary suspect. Knight's attorneys were not made aware of this affidavit, which would have discredited Becker on the stand and proved he was committing perjury by lying under oath about the real purpose of his visit to Compton and his subsequent encounter with Anderson.

Worse still, Knight's attorneys were unaware of the search warrant affidavit which contradicted Detective Becker's sworn testimony because the Los Angeles District Attorney's office had buried it. When asked on record by the Judge about the existence of the affidavit, according to Knight's appeal, "The trial court asked the prosecutor on the record whether the People possessed any (impeachment) material relevant to the probation violation or sentencing proceedings. The prosecutor answered the people possessed no such material." As a result, Judge Czugeler had denied a discovery motion Knight's attorneys had filed based on their suspicions concerning the authenticity of Detective Becker. Even Judge Czugeler himself doubted much of Becker's testimony, yet he allowed it to stand as credible evidence that Anderson was lying for Knight. As detailed in Knight's appeal filing, "The judge conducting the probation revocation hearing stated on the record he did not believe Becker's testimony...The Judge characterized...Becker's testimony as 'pretty silly' and noted the fact that Becker's lying...should have been 'pretty obvious to everyone'." Political pressure had clearly governed the Judge's decision, as most courts would have immediately dismissed the entirety of any witness's testimony where obvious perjury was involved, in line with the Supreme Court case law, such as United States vs. Agurs, where they held that "a conviction obtained by the knowing use of perjured testimony is fundamentally unfair and must be set aside if there is 'any reasonable likelihood that the false testimony could have affected the judgment of the (trier of fact)'."

The Supreme Court in their ruling against Knight's appeal also rejected the notion that Becker's testimony would have had any great impact on the outcome of the hearing, even though they also refer to the Detective's testimony as *false*, still nevertheless ruling that "the defect in Knight's argument is that in this case there was no reasonable likelihood that Becker's false testimony could have affected the outcome of the hearing." If Becker's testimony had been thrown out, the prosecution would have had no witness to refute Anderson's testimony that Knight was helping him rather than trying to hurt him in the course of the attack. The event captured on the MGM video was the principle piece of evidence used to argue that Knight had violated his probationary terms by participating in an altercation.

Without Detective Becker, the court was left with the testimony of Knight and Anderson. To argue then that Becker's testimony had no real bearing on the outcome of the hearing is ludicrous, and in complete violation of Knight's civil rights. In addition to Detective Becker's lying on the stand about the nature of his visit into Anderson's neighborhood in the first place, Knight also took issue in his appeal with the manner in which Detective Becker went about obtaining Orlando Anderson's statement that contradicted his in-court testimony at the revocation hearing. Principally, Knight's appeal argued that the statement had been elicited via coercion, as Becker did not Mirandize Anderson before beginning to question him about the fight the night of the Shakur murder.

At the hearing, Knight's attorneys had raised objections to the admission of Anderson's statement on the grounds that it had been an involuntary omission, and to no great surprise, Judge Czugeler had kept the corruption train chugging right along, denying Knight's motion and ruling that Knight lacked standing to challenge the credibility of Anderson's statement to Detective Becker based on it's the means by which it was elicited. This, despite the fact that the Supreme Court, in LaFeance v. Bohlinger, had ruled that a "defendant has standing to challenge the use of a witness's coerced out of court statements for impeachment purposes when the witness recants statements at trial." Clearly, this ruling applied to Anderson's statements at trial in Knight's favor, which clearly contradicted those he had allegedly made to Detective Becker. The Supreme Court, in collusion with the trial court and District Attorney's office, also refused to recognize the US Supreme Court's precedent in the aforementioned matter, ruling that "we find the court's error nonprejudical." Never mind that they had earlier ruled in their response to Knight's appeal that "the trial court erred in ruling Knight lacked standing to challenge the voluntariness of Anderson's statement made while in police custody."

Clearly, Suge Knight should have never been sentenced to the nine year term when the court, as supported by the California State Court of Appeals, had a wide array of sentencing options, as outlined in the original trial judge's statement that, should Knight violate the terms of his probation, he would be subject to "the range" of nine years in state prison, leaving open the door for a lesser sentence based on the particular nature of the violation. Further, because Knight's contribution to the MGM brawl had consisted of a single kick, the intention of which was questionable, and not substantiated by either side in any significant way that outweighed the credibility of the other, if Knight had been subject to facing jail time, the year he had spent by that point awaiting his hearing should have been considered ample to qualify Knight for time served.

One of the greatest pieces supporting the latter logic is the federal term of two months Knight recently finished serving in the summer of 2001 based on a violation of his federal probation for gun possession charges stemming from the same incident captured on the MGM security video. Certainly, a year would have been more than sufficient for any normal defendant. In addition to his argument that the trial court had a range of sentencing options, based in part on the fact that the initial trial judge had not passed sentence, but, by his own order, had in fact had stated that "imposition of sentence is suspended. The defendant is placed on formal probation for a period of five years." For Knight to be subject to the full nine year term with no flexibility as to alternative options of a lesser severity in length, the court would have had to have formally imposed sentence, rather than suspend its imposition, a crucial distinction which the trial judge failed to ever clearly establish.

Nevertheless, the Supreme Court ruled that "because we have concluded the judge at the probation and sentencing hearing imposed sentence and suspended its execution, the court properly determined that after revoking probation it was required under Howard to order into effect the judgment previously imposed: nine years in prison." That a court of law would ignore gross due process violations such as they did in Knight's case is disturbing in any scenario, but more so when the motive behind it supports an ugly tradition on the part of our government of compromising the rights of African Americans in positions of power and influence. Because Knight had been subject to suborned police testimony and egregious trial errors on the part of the trial judge, which a Court of Appeals later affirmed, in the course of his conviction is even more startling.

Suge Knight was clearly a man with some history of violence, but the majority of his convictions were incidental, not random and impulsive as Los Angeles DA William Hodgman had argued. That the trial court went along with framing Knight in that light is even more chilling, as it proved him in collusion with Gil Garcetti's ugly campaign. Pandering to the cameras and to his political superiors, Judge Czugeler had characterized Knight as a danger to his community, despite the fact that many of Los Angeles' most prominent inner-city civic leaders had come to speak on Suge's behalf as a caring and overly-generous contributor toward the betterment of that very community he was supposedly a threat to.

In the end, Suge Knight lost. Like many other prominent African American leaders in our nation's ugly history of racism, once Knight became a threat to the establishment, it was over. Once Gil Garcetti had determined that Knight was his election year lamb, there was no way to avoid being sacrificed. That was exactly how Suge would go on to view his subsequent incarceration, as something unjust and involuntary, but necessary in the course of the people's struggle. The groundwork he had laid during his meteoric rise to the top of the pop charts would resonate in the hearts of Death Row's core fan base, keeping the label afloat through an incredible trek of adversity that would include federal investigations into allegations of money laundering and drug dealing, fraud, countless civil suits and IRS audits, and accusations of murder.

None would ever be substantiated, and in some ways, the allegations worked to keep Death Row's notoriety from dulling too dramatically. For Suge, who was directly forbidden from operating a business while serving his prison term, his spirit would continue to guide Death Row's course, and as each of the label's remaining stars abandoned ship on the captain they had once revered like a father, Suge would, as Death Row's publicity team put it, continue to "eat off" their plates even as they moved on in their respective careers with other labels. This came, principally, as a result of the complete autonomy Suge had maintained over Death Row's Master Catalog, such that his foresight regarding its long-term value would spell itself out for the world as Death Row continued to score top 20 chart positions with the majority of its releases during the four years Suge was incarcerated.

These included five top 5 Billboard albums, including four posthumous Tupac Shakur releases, a Death Row compilation album aptly titled *The Chronic 2000: Suge Knight Represents,* and a movie soundtrack to *Gang Related.* Moreover, through long term contracts Suge had signed with Death Row's marquee artists, including Snoop Dogg, Tupac, and the Dogg Pound, he continued to participate financially in their releases, both through Death Row's release of various artist albums composed primarily of unreleased material, and through partnerships with other labels who now handled former Death Row's artists. In securing their releases from Death Row Records, the artist had to agree to pay Death Row royalties from future releases by those artists, principally Snoop Dogg, as he moved on to Master P's No Limit Records following his departure from Death Row. For many of Suge's competitors, there seemed to exist a collective relief that Knight was no longer a threat, or at least not an immediate one. And with his label's lifeline safely intact, Suge's journey over the next four years, between the remainder of 1996 and 2001, proved to be a deeply personal one of reckoning and revitalization of the spirit. Suge would find himself in prison, and in doing so, redefine his vision for Death Row's direction in the coming millennium.

Chapter 9

All in the Family

Where Suge Knight publicly held Death Row Records out in concept, from its infancy, as almost a mafia-style family of criminally affiliated gang members who had gone legitimate by joining Knight's organization, but whose presence maintained an authenticity that could not be manufactured or recreated in any other manner in the course of achieving what Suge truly sought to in the expansion of Death Row. The label's culture was one of tough love, where loyalty prevailed over all else.

As Snoop Dogg remembered in his early days with Death Row, the atmosphere was a close knit one in which being a member of the family was almost the equivalent of being blood relatives, literally in terms of the life long membership code that governed many of the labels' employees, who applied their gang mentality in the workplace, such that, according to Snoop, "back when I was on Death Row….if a nigga wanted to leave, ma'fuckas would have the attitude like, 'This nigga's a bitch. Fuck that nigga.'… When niggas wanted to leave Death Row, there was violence and there was beef. They ran Death Row like a street company." As the label grew, so too did the family concept expand to include an elaborate entourage of non-essential personnel, outside of possibly serving to maintain the label's gangsta-friendly image and authenticity. With Knight managing this gangland conglomerate, their issue of overpopulation had been contained. Publicly, Death Row prided itself on the notion that its doors, and in essence, pocketbook, were open to anyone who had come from the same inner city neighborhoods of Compton where Knight had grown up, and were seeking to move up without necessarily moving on from the culture. This was a central ingredient of its formula for maintaining a platinum trend with the millions of Death Row fans who ate Knight's concept up.

In short, Suge had taken the middleman out of the equation in feeding surburban America's craving for a real dose of inner city reality to cure the boredom that traditionally accompanied the safety of an upper-class upbringing. With the same stone, he was using the millions of dollars in proceeds from his label's success in satisfying the aforementioned hunger among record buyers to revitalize traditionally impoverished neighborhood economies by providing hundreds of jobs for young African American gang members and ex-convicts who might otherwise have no legitimate options of employment available to them, and be forced to resort to the criminal enterprises that Death Row made its name glorifying in an O.G. capacity. Death Row worked because Suge argued that his people had already put in their time. Death Row marquee artists like Snoop Dogg had been convicted felons. Knight himself had a lengthy and well-documented record of criminal convictions.

Suge loved his community, and so too did the rest of hip hop record buying America. Such that, at the height of the East Coast/West Coast conflict, Suge suggested it could be resolved through a charity boxing match between Bad Boy Records and Death Row, wherein the proceeds would go directly back into Compton, without any buffers: "What I think we should do is have a charity match (between Tupac and Puffy, and Suge and Biggy) and give the money right back to the ghetto." Suge continued to put his money where his mouth was even after he was incarcerated, in December of 2000, after watching a news report about an inner city elementary school playground that had been vandalized, Suge called Death Row from behind bars and ordered a check cut for upward of $20,000 and made out directly to the school to cover the entirety of the repair costs.

Bottom line: with Suge's love for his community, there were no middlemen. Even his every effort to invest money back into the community, Suge sought to avoid conventional channels like tax deductible donations or related corporate gifts. He preferred a hands-on approach that kept both of his feet firmly rooted in the neighborhoods of his youth. He never veered from adhering strictly to their rules of conduct either, going so far as to buy his childhood home from his parents when he moved them into a wealthier suburb of Los Angeles after Death Row had taken off. In describing the nature of the workforce that composed Death Row's organization, Suge had once explained that "we called it Death Row 'cause most everybody had been involved with the law...A majority of our people were parolees or incarcerated—it's no joke."

As the label's influence in pop music became more expansive as the early nineties unfolded, while Suge looked outward in the potential audiences he could reach with his reality rap conglomerate, within Death Row's inner sanctum, Knight had begun to sculpt a more narrowly-defined interpretation of his notion of family, that is, extending its definition only to blood relatives who he knew he could trust implicitly to help manage the label's growth as it flourished into a pop phenomenon. This began with Suge making his wife, Sharitha Knight, manager of Snoop Dogg, the label's most popular rising star. Knight also employed his brother in law, Norris Anderson, a man who Suge had known for ten years prior, and held absolute trust in. First hired as a low-level receptionist, Anderson quickly moved his way up Death Row's short ladder to the position of general manager, becoming one of Suge's most trusted confidants.

While Knight's consolidation of his inner circle to include principally family members does not suggest Suge second-guessing himself with respect to who he could trust within his very extended family, he at the very least had begun to believe in setting different tiers for the level of that trust. In short, as time went on and the label grew more successful, the higher you went, the more responsibility you had, and therein, the closer to Suge you had to be. Knight, by 1994, had begun insulating himself, as Norris Anderson suspected, because "as Suge built this company, his family was not really involved for a very long time. Then there came a point where he sought out his family to see if they wanted to come into the business. I'm sure there was a reason for that."

One logical reason for the latter was simply that, as Death Row grew, it did so as a result of its million-strong image, such that, after a certain point, Suge could not voluntarily shrink from the monstrosity he had created without

risking the hip hop community viewing the move as hypo-
critical. Death Row had become a massive clique, and Suge
was its most popular member, both among his gang-affiliated peers and in the media. To avoid risking an erosion of
his concept of the Death Row family, Suge at its core made
the wise decision to insulate himself by keeping only those
he could consider real family close to him. As his brother-
in-law joked matter of factly in explaining the literal definition of the latter strategy on Knight's part to help qualify
it, "see, I'm Suge's brother-in-law...I marries his sister...
I've known him for 20 years. I've known his sister for 20
years, and we've been married for 10 years. Its just like...
well, I'm part of the family...I've come along way (at
Death Row), I started out answering phones. That's a long
way."

By teaching his brother-in-law the business to the point
where Anderson eventually acceded to the position of general manager of the label, by the time Suge was incarcerated, his foresight had come full circle, and its implied
strategy kicked in without skipping much of a beat. As
Anderson recalled upon Suge's initial incarceration in LA
County Jail, Death Row's staff handled the transition
because they knew the order of the hierarchy intimately,
and trusted in its chain of command, from Suge, down to
this brother-in-law, and so forth, such that when his probation was first revoked, "Suge was still the man at the con-
trols...I was in contact with him: he made the decisions,
and I made sure they were carried out."

Throughout the course of the following year, as Death
Row's life-without-Suge began to take form, in the midst
of IRS audits, multi-million civil dollar lawsuits, ATF-F.B.I.
investigations, and the eminent reality of Suge's long-term
incarceration, Death Row's staff stuck together because it

was composed of family, and in concept, this had always been the core of Suge's philosophy for survival. As Anderson speculated on the label's coming struggles during the first year following Knight's initial incarceration, as the wolves began to circle Death Row's wounded incarnation, Anderson's outlook for survival was rooted very much in Suge's concept of a bonded family: "I don't think its going to be smooth for us...We have a whole lot of adversity ahead...But I think its something we can overcome. Suge always preached family, and he's always preached that we needed to stick together. If they divide us, quite naturally they will conquer us. Everybody here realizes that. So when it comes down to the nitty-gritty, everybody stocks together. I've seen it time and again."

Loyalty would definitely be central to Death Row surviving the next four years of adversity that would follow. The first member of Death Row's inner family to jump ship was franchise rapper Snoop Dogg, who left in mid-1997, less than a year into Suge's formal incarceration, because, as he grimly put it, "there's nothing over there. Suge Knight is in jail, the president; Dr. Dre left and Tupac is dead. Its telling me that I'm either gong to be dead or in jail or I'm going to be nothing."

In truth, Snoop's departure was not that simple, but nevertheless a crippling blow for the label as it adjusted to life without Suge at the helm. Snoop's follow up to *Doggy Style* had garnered lackluster sales, due in part to the absence of Dr. Dre at the production helm. As a result, the record moved a respectable two million copies, but fell far short of the 6 million copies its predecessor, *Doggy Style*, had done at retail. Additionally, Death Row had begun recouping against Snoop's five million dollar legal bill which had resulted from his first degree murder acquittal a year earlier. That the victory had been financed entirely on Suge's dime worked to legally justify the label's position in ceasing to pay Snoop while it collected against the debt did not calm the label's only remaining marquee superstar. As a result, the sentiment between the two parties grew all the more sour as months passed, and Snoops' bills mounted. By the time he invoked a California State law which allows for the dissoluton of any contract following seven years of employment, and left the Suge-less Death Row Records for Master P's booming No Limit Records camp, he was sitting on a million dollar IRS debt, among a mountain of other debt.

While Snoop's commercial revitalization in the hip hop press, promulgated entirely as a result of his signing with red hot Master P, he sought to play down on his previous vehemence against Death Row and Knight, Snoop still seemed unsure of himself in his feelings toward Suge, preferring a more diplomatic route at the suggestions of Master P. Where in one interview Snoop claimed that had Suge not been incarcerated, he might very well have stayed with the label, in other interviews, he took a more stand-offish position, praising Master P for breaking him "free from those suckas on Death Row...After...Snoop Dogg left, Death Row Records saw their fall....We actually bounced out of that situation and eventually became even more successful than we would've become under Death Row Records."

Snoop's type of tongue lashing at Suge is exactly the type of rhetoric that began to fly rampant at the label following Knight's incarceration. Afeni Shakur filed a multi-million dollar lawsuit alleging multiple counts of fraud, to which the eventual result was an out of court settlement which included a preliminary $3 million dollar payment to Afeni

Shakur by Interscope on Death Row's behalf, along with an eventual award to the Shakur Estate of control of 150 of the 200 masters that Tupac had recorded in his eight months with the label. While Death Row maintained partial ownership of the tracks, and received royalty payments from album sales the songs generated, the ruling was still regarded as a stinging slap in the face to Suge personally, who had considered Tupac his best friend and the equivalent of his little brother at the time of his death, remarking sadly that "I'm not mad, but I'm disappointed at Tupac's mother. While I'm incarcerated, people tell her that the songs I paid for and marketed is her songs. And she made statements saying that (Tupac) never got any money. I got signed documents where he received over $2.5 million, even before he was supposed to receive any money. And beyond all that, when he was incarcerated, I gave his mother $3 million."

Though Suge and Afeni would eventually resolve their differences enough to co-executive produce and release three post-humous Tupac albums, a Greatest Hits collection, and two double albums, the damage done to Suge's reputation, and that of the label, during the first years of his incarceration would have been devastating were it not for Suge's centered perspective and his loyal staff's determination to keep the label above continually choppy waters.

As Death Row was a label built in the face of a great tradition of adversity, so too it fought on as 1997 ended and 1998 began. In response to public attacks from former artists like Snoop Dogg, Death Row struck back by repeatedly dissing the artist on label compilations including *The Chronic 2000: Suge Knight Represents, Death Row's Greatest Hits,* and *Too Gangster for Radio,* their most scathing attack on Snoop came with the release of a Snoop solo album consisting of unreleased material that Knight controlled, vengefully titled *Dead Man Walking*, implying through its title that Snoop was a traitor who would never be the star he had been under Knight's tutelage. Additionally, because of the long term contract Snoop had signed with Death Row prior to his departure, wherein he still owed the label seven full-length albums, Suge had secured financial participation in all of Snoop's future releases up through the fulfillment of the Death Row contract. Aside from planning a forthcoming *Greatest Hits* album of Snoop Dogg's Death Row era material, the label also retaliated to Snoop's interviews dissing Knight and company with continual taunts of their own, notably including the label's leaking of Snoop's 2000 No Limit release, *The Last Meal*, symbolic in title as it was the third and final album of his deal with Master P, whereafter Snoop planned to release albums solely via his own imprint, Dogg House Records.

In an effort to remind Snoop that he was still obligated to Knight, i.e. a prisoner on Death Row if he chose not to be a willing inmate, the label offered both their own *Dead Man Walking* and Snoop's "The Last Meal" for free download off the Death Row website for the purposes of comparison. When Snoop, No Limit Records, and Priority Records threatened legal action, Suge countered with an argument that was sound from Death Row's position, but only worked to further taunt Snoop, wherein Knight reasoned that he had no cause to stifle Snoop's album sales when he participated financially in their sales. When Snoop's own release debuted at number one on Billboard's Top 200 pop chart, Death Row taunted Snoop with ads the label ran in the *Source* and *Vibe* congratulating Snoop on the success of The Last Meal, and reminding him that "Death Row Records knows that success for a Snoop Dogg album means $$$$ for Suge Knight. Keep it up because you know Suge Knight eats off your next three albums as well as your previous seven albums!!!" Suge himself had slyly and correctly predicted the latter when he had agreed to release Snoop from his contract three years prior in 1997, remarking that "I'm gonna be making money off Snoop for a long time to come." While in prison, Suge had the luxury of sitting back and watching the interest role in on his investment in Snoop, without having to lift a finger in the process. Simply, Suge joked in a who-me fashion, "I'm in the penitentiary. The only thing that I do is my time. I'm quite sure that Death Row will be putting out (future Snoop releases)." For all Snoop's whining in the press, there was little he could do about it.

While Death Row continued to have a healthy chart positioning and sales trend with their releases, which they drew principally from their existing Master vault of unreleased artist material, Interscope Records severed ties with the label in 1998, and following a brief period with Priority Records as distributor, Death Row eventually settled into a solid but less glamorous deal with respected independent distributor DNA Music Distribution. Though the label's Tupac releases were handled by major labels, as the masters were co-owned by Afeni's Amaru Records, which is distributed through Jive Records, the transition from corporate independent back to what in essence was a truly independent label may have been the best move Death Row made in its Knight-behind-bars era.

Aside from allowing the label more room to breathe with its release schedule commitments, the move to DNA was an practical adjustment and honest acknowledgement of where the label truly stood in the ever-evolving hip hop climate, which was now ruled by East Coast imprints like

Def Jam,, who featured DMX and Jay Z, and southern independents like Master P's No Limit Records and Cash Money Records, which featured Juvenile. Suge agreed with this transition, as he took a level-headed approach to the fact that while he was in jail, his label was realistically limited in what new moves it could make. West Coast Rap was very much an underground movement now, and in this definition, Death Row Records was still on the front lines, signing renowned underground rappers like Swoop G, Crooked I, who had previously been signed to Virgin Records, and Big Hutch aka Cold 187 Um from veteran NWA-era rap group Above the Law. The label was clearly in a rebuilding process, very much in line with the current trends as they pertained to West Coast hip hop. As he elaborated on the label's strategy in one jail-house interview, Suge reaffirmed the label's revised marketing approach for new releases, confirming that "they know how I like it done, one release at a time."

While Death Row weathered an industry storm on one front, on another Suge Knight battled a host of allegations concerning his true intentions in operating Death Row, that is, to become a hip hop powerhouse, or to serve as a money laundering operation for drug profits earned in the Blood's street narcotics trade. Though an extensive investigation was conducted by a federal grand jury, no formal charges were ever filed against Suge in the matter. In responding to the allegations, Suge has sought to play the charges out in the media as old fashioned, institutionalized racism coated in complex, politically charged legal jargon, wherein he theorizes that while "I wouldn't say it's a conspiracy…(but) when I went to prison, it should have been a wake up call for people in the industry…I'm a businessman, an entrepreneur…I'm from the ghetto…But I'm not the bad guy that I'm made out to be. When you take a stand on line in America, do things your way and own your own, that can be scary for people"

More horrific, however, were the charges lodged by the Los Angeles Police Department against Knight in early 1998 that he was being considered a prime suspect in the murder of Bad Boys franchise rapper Notorious B.I.G. In a *Rolling Stone* feature on the allegations, which stopped just short of accusing Knight directly of ordering the murder, the charge is outlined as one in which, according to the article, by author Randall Sullivan, entitled "The Murder of the Notorious B.I.G.—Suge Knight, gangster cops and allegations of police cover-up: the shocking story behind L.A.'s most famous unsolved crime and the whistle-blower who wants to set the record straight." In the article, former LAPD officer Russell Poole, outlines his own theories and conclusions about the motive for Biggie Smalls' murder and what he alleges is Suge's involvement in masterminding the murder. Poole's conspiracy theory also drew in the scandal within Los Angeles's Rampart Division, involving police misconduct and gang members.

Despite the fact that *Rolling Stone* based their story on the claims of a fired police detective who was removed from the BIG investigation, Death Row issued the following statement regarding the story shortly following its publication, "Mr. Knight is completing an analysis of the *Rolling Stone Magazine* article and statements made in the article to the writer Randall Sullivan by ex-Los Angeles police officer, Russell Poole, regarding Mr. Knight and the LAPD's Rampart Division, in order to ascertain any lawful and legal remedies that may be available to him in this matter. Mr. Knight, Mr. Kenner and Mr. Wright will review the article with their attorneys, David Chesnoff and Donald Re, to point out the many inaccuracies contained therein.

The allegations in the article are denied as ridiculous and absurd. It should be noted that the Chief of the LAPD, Bernard Parks, was recently quoted as believing the Rampart case has been exploited by the media and police critics and is being 'distorted beyond all proportion,' and also that, according to Chief Parks, 'Officer Poole had some theories that could not be substantiated. He only brought it up when he left the department and after he had been personally disciplined and removed from the task force.'"

Suge took issue first hand with the allegations that he had anything to do with BIG's murder, taking the position that it would have been an impossibility given his incarceration, and arguing "why would I try to do something to him? Who knows? Maybe one day he could have been signed to Death Row. I don't know why mothafuckas tryin' to pin that on me. I don't even know the mothafucka they tried to connect me with. Anybody with any kind of sense know I wasn't involved. Anytime you have somebody doing positive stuff and just doing their time and minding their own business, people will sit up there and lie. I never seen no shootin'. I only know what I heard and what I read. I had no involvement." Suge has even gone so far as to argue that the allegations lodged against him regarding the BIG slaying have plagued his chances at an early release from prison, as "they were ready to let me out of prison until Biggie was shot, then they put the judgment on hold...I was never accused of having anything to do with it...but I (was) still stuck in jail."

Personally, Suge seemed deep into his incarceration to have made peace with his rival Sean Puffy Combs, remarking in the midst of Comb's gun possession trial that, despite their past rivalry, "I don't want to see Puff Daddy go to prison. He's not a friend of mine, but I definitely don't want to see him go to prison. One thing about prison is its not made for everybody...I've known Puffy from before he started Bad Boy, when he was at Uptown. Puffy's always been a good guy...Puffy's a nice guy. The way the media portrays him as this tough guy, this street guy, which he's not. For him to go to prison?...I think it would be wrong for him to go to prison for the simple fact that he would be so much of a victim. He's a small guy, he's a guy who obviously...the people that are incarcerated are gonna look at him as just a guy with money. He's small...and they gonna try to take advantage of him. Another reason I don't want to see him in prison is...that the guy has got two kids...God gives you certain...challenges to conquer in your life because there's a lot of tests...For Puffy...hopefully it works out for him. See, I'm not bitter. I'm not bitter at nobody....If I got a problem with Puffy, that's a personal problem with me and him. Which I don't." While Suge's sympathy toward Puffy is still rooted somewhat in the notion on Knight's part that his relationship with Puffy is something of a David vs. Goliath complex.

In a *Newsweek* interview, Suge took a bolder stance on the issue, bringing it back into the arena of Death Row's superiority over Bad Boy, i.e. Knight's over Combs, joking that "they don't send a nigga who's wearing shiny suits and hanging out with Martha Stewart to jail," said Knight of the artist who changed his moniker to "P. Diddy... Who is he a threat to? He's just acting a fool. I'm the nigga people are afraid of." Suge has also used the press's interest regarding his positions on Puffy's trial to revive the notion that a competition still exists between the two labels, reminiscent of the heyday of the East Coast/West Coast beef, but without the violence that plagued the feud, such that "I'd like to see the guy back out doing records 'cause one thing about the music business is, the better the competition, the better it makes you work. If you put out a good record, that makes you put out an even better record, cause you have competition (That's the) one thing about it is, what made all of us better was the competition. I know when I'm...out there—I don't care who it is—if they put out a great record, I'm going to be in the studio that night."

Without the glare of the media, or the record sales potential based on their inflation of what began as a personal beef between Tupac Shakur and Notorious BIG, Suge has distinguished many of the controversial fires within himself in quest for a personal perspective regarding his situation, which he very possibly has come full circle in reaching. Referring to prison as a place where "I've grown mentally, physically, and spiritually", Suge has strived to let go many of the demons that worked to put him behind bars in the first place. This baptism began with Suge's acknowledgement of his own role in the circumstances that landed him behind bars in the first place, conceding that "I feel I was taught a lesson. One minute I'm running a multi-million dollar business, the next I was in prison and my artists weren't my artists anymore." And with that reality fixed firmly in place before him, Suge began his journey down a path that would allow him time for reflection, rejuvenation of the spirit, and a second chance that not many of his fellow convicts would have upon release.

Chapter 10

Serenity Prayer

Suge Knight and the California Penal System

Marion "Suge" Knight's home from late 1997 through August, 2001, was Mull Creek State Prison, located in Ione, California, roughly 50 miles from Sacramento. While he has previously spent time in prisons including Chino and at the California Men's Colony in San Luis Obispo, Mule Creek State Prison has been Suge's longest stay in one facility during his four-plus years of incarceration. His cell block captain for the last year of his stay in Mule Creek was a stern but friendly man named Sergeant Brown, and for all intents and purposes, Suge remained a model prisoner during his four years of incarceration. Highlights in Knight's mishaps have included relatively minor things like a broken foot injured during a basketball game on the prison yard. He has received a regular influx of visitors during his imprisonment, typically between Thursday through Sunday, including family (his mother Maxine, ex-wife Sharitha, and children, and ex-wife Michelle, whom Suge briefly married while in prison), friends, and current and former business associates including Death Row's former chief council David Kenner, Suge's longtime assistant Roy, Interscope's Jimmy Iovine, Priority's Bryan Turner, Interscope head of sales Steve Berman, promo veteran Marc Benesch, ex-Death Row publicist George Pryce.

The majority of Death Row's current artist roster, including Crooked I and Big Hutch, have paid Suge visits at one time or another, as have a select handful of reporters, including journalists from *Newsweek*, and hip hop staples *Rap Pages* and *The Source*, whose reporter described Mull Creek State Prison more elaborately in the course of his article as "a nondescript stretch of land just across the street from a modern, gated development built around a golf course, with houses that would probably fetch half a million back in L.A. The only signs it's not a community college campus are the empty gun turrets rising like forbidding beacons above the barren, treeless landscape, the electronic fence with the sign, 'Warning! Fatal Shock,' and the coiled barbed wire snaking around the top."

A long way from the plush Beverly Hills and Can Am headquarters Knight once occupied at the helm of Death Row Records, he settled into prison life remarkably well, according to most associates and friends, as well as Knight himself, who views the situation in retrospect as a lesson for the next generation of African American youth to learn from. That aside, Suge seems more intent on looking toward the future than dwelling on his four years in prison, "I don't want to talk about the past because we can't change it. We have to move forward and give these new kids the opportunity to reach their own goals."

Part of moving forward for Knight involved first acknowledging the role that his fast-lane lifestyle contributed to the
predicament he ended up in. Suge had vowed while in
prison to establish for himself a redirection and focus upon
release that, like the 50+ pounds he shed while locked
down, seeks to get his label back into the heavyweight
champion-esque shape it maintained before his incarceration. Much like two time champion Mike Tyson, whom
Death Row Records has held an affiliation with since its
very early days, the label in its heyday dropped hit records
like Tyson did every opponent that was put in front of him.
The lack of competition, however, according to Suge, made
the label soften a bit, losing its edge as it embraced a notion
of invincibility that extended to almost every facet of its
operation, at one point inspiring Knight at his most arrogant to rename his label **The New and Untouchable Death
Row Records**. Reflecting, Suge recalls that "before I came
in, I hung out at clubs all the time, spent a lot of time on the
streets...When I get home, that's going to change. I'll be
handling my business, making sure it's back on top."

Despite the fact that he has found a balance and temperament within himself, Suge has clearly not lost his ambition,
and is motivated in part out of a vengefulness that seeks to
reclaim his title as the Don of West Coast hip hop, much in
the spirit of Tyson, as both titles remained vacant during
each man's incarceration. Moreover, Knight, applying his
all-boy philosophy, clearly holds a desire to call his adversaries on the novel full of trash talking they have done in
the press about him over the course of his four-year incarceration. Upon receiving the news that he would be
granted a release date shortly into the summer of 2001,
Suge boasted with a mix of a 10 year old's glee at the sight
of his new bike and the trademark gusto that slain hip-hip
prodigal son Tupac Shakur traditionally displayed in the

media. "I got a release date and I'm coming home. I know a lot of niggas are scared, but time went so fast. When I come home, I want all those people who was talking shit about me to be able to look me in my eye and say the same things. People afraid of Suge…They been callin up here, asking when I am gonna get out. When I hit bricks, it all belongs to me."

Long before Suge would be granted his imminent release from a prison term that had been handed down much to the relief of an industry of onlookers who had held their breath during Knight's six year reign at the helm of West Coast hip hop, waiting to see when the balloon would get too big and be forced to pop. The record industry had traditionally behaved in their dealings with Death Row Records like a 16 year old cheerleader in a movie who was too enthralled and numb with both fear and desire to discern one from the other in surrendering to the advances of a seductive high school football star. Even if they had wanted to say no to Knight, they could not via a combination of trepidation at the thought of facing Knight's towering intimidation and awe in the presence of Death Row's star power, via artists like Tupac and Snoop Dogg.

It wasn't that they sat by and did nothing, rather they were collectively paralyzed with an identical apprehension and equal want to be part of something as both raw and real as the product Knight's company put out. When he was first imprisoned, Suge himself was faced with the prospect of living up to his own reputation in the face of authentic gangstas—convicts who, as newspapers traditionally speculate concerning the treatment of celebrity prisoners by fellow inmates, would have immediately sought to make Knight a mark. Not surprisingly, prison only served to further authenticate the reality of Knight's character as the hardest inmate locked down on Death Row. Immediately, there were tabloid reports swirling that Knight had been the victim of a stabbing (rumored to have been arranged by Michael Harry O Harris, as retribution for the money Knight had allegedly screwed him out of).

Additionally, another journalist reported that, despite Knight's active status as a member of the Bloods street gang, he had paid protection money to both factions, the Bloods and the Crips, to ensure his safety while inside. As it turned out, none of the aforementioned were true. Instead, Suge got by on his own authenticity among convicts, who, as it turned out, seemed to respect Knight for being the real thing. As Suge himself confirmed in explaining why he had no problems on the inside of prison walls, he was the amongst the same crowd on the streets or behind bars, wherein "with me, (prison) made me stronger. One thing about me is that, it's sad to say…any prison I go to, it's going to be 20, 30 or 40 guys from my neighborhood there, because most of my people where I grew up at end up incarcerated."

Moreover, Suge took prison first as an opportunity to shed himself of Death Row groupies, the first step toward cleansing himself of those elements of his past that had helped put him in prison in the first place. This is not to say that he abandoned his criminal affiliations with fellow gang members, rather that he grew closer to a definition of true loyalty among his family and business associates alike, where "in prison, you get the chance to see who really loves you. That little buck gives you a lot of time to think." In elaborating on what being incarcerated did to sharpen Suge's skills at sizing up both his current and future competition, he brings the notion of succeeding at anything back down to a basic level that seems almost improbable given the heights he had seemingly fallen from in his transition from CEO to convict.

Nevertheless, Suge's resilience in the course of his four-year incarceration is rooted in his firm belief a play-the-card-you're-dealt philosophy that succeeds by remaining grounded, whether sitting in a prison cell or behind an oak desk in a high-rise office. Such that, as Suge chose to apply it, he looked at his sentence as a challenge with a potential for street-smart upsides that he highlights to include "(making you) a better judge of character. Like, if you take an artist or so-called friend or whoever, if they don't a have a good heart or they're not really your friend, you don't have to waste your time bullshittin' with 'em. You pick up on people much faster. In less than five minutes, you can have a conversation with somebody and tell if the person is a snake or he full of shit. There is a difference between me and most, which is that I am fresh off the block. I don't look for no special privileges. I'm a man who paid my dues. No person ever gave me nothing but God. Like I said before, a lot of these Black guys go into these record labels tap dancin' and shakin' they ass to get in the door. One thing nobody can ever take from me is that I never been on no records, poppin' around in no videos or shakin' my ass. I don't be no cheerleader. I come in like a businessman and I do business. I make sure that the people around me have the success that I have. And that's not that Hollywood success. I don't care about how many times somebody recognizes my face. My thing was to be the man who makes his little 30 or 40 million a year and still get a cheeseburger and fries and don't worry about an autograph."

Unlike most, Knight over his four years in prison employed a unique formula by which he kept both prison and the record industry linked, possibly because the media continually explored the complexities of Knight's charisma and menace, writing enough speculative "What will become of Death Row?" pieces to rival those authored about what the future holds for an elusive N.W.A. reunion. In seeking to explain his own perspective on the independent variable in what could become of Death Row upon his release vs. the fixed limbo the label remains in while the world waits out Knight's parole date, Suge largely disregard the notion that his experience should be looked at as anything more than an example of what happens daily to African American males adversely and unfairly pegged by a racist system. In his eyes, what happened to him is very much a byproduct of overzealous prosecution based on Knight's African American celebrity and fear by the white establishment of the implications of that power's reach potential. Its root however, is simply old fashion racism, and as such, Knight chose not to overly-politicize it, but handle the experience as simply as any other African American who was unjustly convicted of a crime might handle the transition from the freedom and responsibility of their every day life to one where your exposure to the sunshine, let alone any other enlightment, is controlled by men with firearms.

To that end, he cites initial perspective going into the situation he did as key to surviving its aftermath as that reality sinks in. Knight used his acceptance of the circumstance as the beginning to a journey toward establishing a serenity within himself that he may not have ever considered possible given his position as CEO of hip hop's most volatile and successful independent label. As he simplified it, "you go in, you get sentenced, you do your time…I had no time to reflect before. Jail is the worst place you can be, but it does give you an opportunity to grow, to focus on what's important. It's good to get all this rest, not have your phone or pager constantly going off. I've found peace." In summarizing his personal disposition entering the nine year period of incarceration Suge faced, he chose to view himself as very much removed from the situation, aside from reconciling personally the role he played in affecting the end his situation did. Knight seems to take more issue with the means toward that end, chalking it up to something inevitable, for a variety of reasons he would spend the four years exploring—"It's like my grandmother said, 'Whatever hand you're dealt, that's what you have to deal with.' You can't justify what goes on in life…Prison is a place nobody wants to be…I view this as God making me a man, testing me."

Outside the walls of Knights soul and those of the prison that held him, the rest of the world moved on. Dr. Dre and Snoop Dogg continued their careers, recovering from the transitional period of readjustment that followed leaving the platinum guarantees Death Row's umbrella had provided. Snoop Dogg shortened his name to Snoop Dogg, at Master P's behest, and released a trilogy of albums in three years time, the exact number required under the terms of his deal with Master P, who chose the role of the diplomat in his dealings with Knight in the course of signing Snoop. According to Master P, who when he approached Knight about securing Snoop's release, kept things on a strictly-business level, essentially avoiding the beef between the two men by agreeing to everything Knight demanded in his relinquishment of Snoop's contract: "I went in…and asked him what he wanted, and that was it." Suge himself has said nothing negative about Master P in the press, reserving his criticisms for Snoop himself, who he has repeatedly likened to a traitor and a pop sell-out who, by leaving Death Row when he did, lost any remaining street credibility he may have had with hard core hip hop fans.

While Snoop's first two albums on Master P's No Limit label were definitely fast food offerings (the first recorded in 3 weeks time) in comparison to his two albums released on Death Row, his career has made a solid rebound from the period immediately following the commercial failure of *Tha Dogg Father*, his last authorized release on Death Row. This rehabilitation has largely been attributed to his re-teaming with Dr. Dre, who has experienced something of a career renaissance of his own since settling soundly into his new position as CEO of Aftermath Entertainment. In the past three years, since early 1999 with the release of white rap phenomenon Eminem, who is something of a Dre protégé, and signed to his label, has won three Grammys and released three multiplatinum albums, including his own comeback solo LP, *The Chronic 2001*, not including countless radio hits he has produced in a one-off capacity for other hip hop stars. Knight has likened both Snoop and Dre to retirees who, with the exception of Dre in a production role, have become saturated by the mainstream success they experienced absent Knight, where in each artist's respective Death Row heyday Suge stood one step behind as a shadow, ensuring both Snoop and Dre maintained an authentic street credibility within their artistry's inevitably commercial cross-over, such that, Suge argues he is more at peace than either Snoop or Dre could possibly be, even with each at the height of their respective careers, "I'm in prison. But my heart and mind is free. Gangsta haters on the streets are doing more time than me. They need 30 police escorts with them every time they walk down the street."

Whatever Suge's role in his own situation, he appears to have to come to terms with it. In doing so, he emerges embodying an authenticity that both of his former marquee rappers could only dream of, along with the majority of hip hop's elite, constantly on a quest to prove or improve their street credibility. Suge has avoided any need for a struggle to maintain his, and has backed it up by handling his time as a human being first, reasoning that "If you are mortal, you make mistakes. But when someone puts a period behind something, why put a question mark? I look at it like this: Whatever I needed to learn, I've learned. I know I'm wiser, smarter, more disciplined, stronger and more spiritual. I've grown for the better. I don't stay the same; I don't thrive on the negative."

One of the only apparent challenges for Suge while incarcerated, though a monumental one for any parent, has been contending with the affects his public image has had within his own family, who he holds sacred and has always maintained a maximum-security lockdown with in the press. Very few photos of Suge's children or his wife have ever seen the light of day in the media, but he has elaborated in some depth on the affects his imprisonment has had on his family, particularly with respect to his children, "People be so quick to judge me as a ghetto muthafucka. They won't let their kids spend the night at my house because I'm supposed to be such a ghetto, violent muthafucka, but my kids get everything they want and are raised well."

Clearly being separated from his family has been one of the hardest elements of Suge's life as a convict, such that he places reuniting with them following his release as more important a priority even than jumpstarting Death Row's stalled engine, "To be honest, I know when I'm coming home. I want to spend time with my family. I don't want a media circus when I get out...I've paid my debt. I won't give anyone the satisfaction of admitting defeat. I'm a better man. I needed to sit back and watch for a while...take a break from the fast lane. I have prayed for the best and prepared for the worst. I'm not counting the days or months until I'm out, because that's hard time. If your friends love and respect you, that's all you can expect." Knight's immediate family has shown an equal affection for the incarcerated Sugarbear, as his mother Maxine affectionately nicknamed him at a small age for his sweet disposition. Today, Maxine Knight is no less doting on Suge, and certainly more defensive regarding his incarceration, remarking that despite Knight's public image, "Suge never gave us any trouble growing up...We knew he'd do whatever he wanted to do because he had charm, and he could charm anyone. He got that from me. (He's in prison because) he's just a rich and powerful black man that people couldn't stand to see succeed."

While in prison, Suge, following his keeping-things-in-simple-perspective principle, has worked to make himself a better person in every facet of his being, which he has referred to not as a rehabilitation, but rather as a rejuvenation of the spirit, body, mind, and quite possibly, the soul. His regimen includes everyman basics, where, according to Suge, "I work, clean my body and sleep. I've been reading some history books, the Bible...that kind of thing." He chooses largely to cook his own meals over a hot plate, and has taken to putting himself through a rigorous workout regimen, prompted in part by what he jokingly remarked to one journalist as his 350 pound belly "hanging out over this little bitty bunk." Suge has shed upward of 50 pounds since his incarceration began in 1996. He has admitted readily to missing the luxuries his millionaire status once afforded him, wherein prison "makes you appreciate what you don't have—a refrigerator, gourmet food. It's going to be wonderful just to have a lobster and a steak." Though his first remark to most every journalist who has peppered him with questions concerning his immediate post-release plans has been much more basic even than luxury cuisine, "The first thing I want to do is take an hour-and-a-half warm bath."

In the end, Suge has found himself in a place most people would be lost, regarding himself as his parole approaches as "passionate about everything, like my family and friends. I am a good judge of character and I only fuck around with my real homies, my real muthafuckas. Anybody that I am talkin' to is gonna be bonafide real. That means that your conversations are better. There is no substitution for happiness. Period."

Chapter 11

"I'm Coming Home!"

O n Monday, August 6, 2001, Marion "Suge" Knight was released from Sheridan Detention Center, in Portland, Oregon, which had been Suge's mystery location in "Federal Custody" since April 20, 2001, when he had been paroled from California state custody after serving over four years for his now-infamous role in the Orlando Anderson beatdown on the night Tupac was mortally wounded. As reported by his hometown paper, the *Los Angeles Times*, Suge boarded a first class flight headed for Los Angeles International Airport, where he was greeted with open arms by his label, Death Row Records, who took him by limo to his company's headquarters in Beverly Hills. Welcomed home by a billboard that had hung by the front of his offices for the entire week preceding his release, displaying Knight's image and a warm, congratulatory **"WELCOME HOME SUGE!"**, Suge seemed to pick up right where he had left off.

In describing his movements first hand following his release Monday morning from Federal custody, Suge seemed intent on following an enthusiastic but routine path that was not bathed in self-pity or any celebration beyond simple indulgences. As he described to a *LA Times* journalist, "The first thing I did when I got off the plane was fire me up a nice cigar...I stopped by a fast food place and got...a cheeseburger and some French fries and a strawberry shake. It felt really good to dig in my pocket and pay for a meal. To press money again felt really good...I didn't come out with the attitude 'Poor me and sorry me, I've been gone five years'...I just picked up like I'd never left...I woke up... and took a nice shower and got dressed and came to my office and went to work and went to the studio and put my energy into music." If Suge himself tried to appear absent of any inflated enthusiasm, his employees at Death Row made sure to pick up the slack with their own excitement, such that he described an atmosphere where "it felt magical to be out of prison, the vibe of the staff, the feeling of home, the new artists. It makes it exciting all over again." True to the theme of family as a central part of his survival mechanism, Suge topped off his first full day out of prison by paying a surprise visit to his mother, Maxine, at 4 am in the morning, where he was greeted by his biggest supporter, "overjoyed with tears," as Suge described her reaction.

Now 36, Knight had truly allowed himself room for a perspective that seemed to make his adjustment psychologically seamless, from his cellblock to Wilshire Boulevard, and his transition from prisoner following orders to CEO handing them out. This was due in large part to Suge's super-human ambition, and to his benefit, the rehabilitated ego that again was acting as his proverbial shadow—in that the rest of the world's outlook was still, to some degree, cast in Suge's past, where he was clearly looking ahead, remarking to *LA Times* journalist Chuck Philips that, "I'm stress free...I'm not bitter. I'm blessed.

I'm glad to be out. I give thanks to God. I want to try to do better things." Answering any lingering doubts concerning Knight's focus, that getting Death Row back on the platinum track it was racing down preceding his incarceration, he didn't talk about kicking back for a few days on the beach, or catching up on female R&R, instead taunting his competition, "you know what they say: 'Demonstration is better than conversation.' Watch me. I'm going to the studio tonight."

Sensing that the world would be watching, Suge has naturally gravitated toward the perpetually curious media attention surrounding Death Row's future. Using the attention surrounding his homecoming to advertise not his, but his label's, return, proclaiming that "better days is coming man!...It's like we're getting ready for the Super Bowl. Preparing for the game. We're going to win the big one. Going to sign some new young producers to come up with some tough new stuff. We going to start having some fun again." That fun commenced the night following Suge's release on Tuesday, August 7, when, after spending the day being chauffeured between business meetings in a black limo, he settled into a night of creativity in the studio with Death Row artists J Valentine and Crooked I, approving final mixes on cuts for both artist's forthcoming albums, elatedly describing the scene to one journalist as a happy mix of business and pleasure, wherein "I celebrated...with making a smash hit on J. Valentine, and finished up a smash hit on Crooked I, who everybody says is the best in the West. They really got me jazzed up and pumped up."

Joking with the same *LA Times* reporter that "it's amazing what...people can say about you when you're in prison," Suge diplomatically sidestepped without underscoring the challenge he had presented his adversaries with while still incarcerated, shortly preceding his release, where he had more boldly challenged that "when I come home, I want all those people who was talkin' shit about me to be able to look me in my eye and say the same things." Suge, the day of his release, took a more political tone regarding his competition, opting instead to pin the importance of Death Row's revitalization to the hopes of a new generation of music fans that would benefit from a comeback, wherein "the next generation is key. I owe them a chance so they don't end up in jail like me. I would never bring harm to kids. Society paints their own vision; they believe what they want to believe."

In truth, it was most probably a healthy mix of the two. Suge has long held a soft spot in his heart for his community, and a true devotion to indulging that affection through countless charitable donations, some in the glare of the media, and others, when publicity couldn't have mattered one way or the other. Notably, including Christmas of 2000, when he had ordered Death Row to pay for the refurbishments of a vandalized playground from his prison cell. In citing children among his fundamental motivations for Death Row's revitalization following his release from prison, it would have been in poor taste to question Knight's voracity or his sincerity toward that end. As he had told one journalist in a prison interview in the spring of 2001 regarding the playground refurbishment, "I grew up in Compton and you only have so long to be a kid. To be deprived of your playground, well, that really touched me, it moved me. I'm just happy I can help. Hey, if I was free and on the streets, I'd be there helping putting the swings and the toys and recreation stuff up." Now that he was free, Suge's eyes were equally focused on reclaiming his heavyweight title, though this time he seemed sincere in his quest to do so in a more dignified manner than he may have the first time. Still, in comparing the two periods for his label, Knight avoided trying to make any excuses for the sometimes brutal methods he had employed in operating Death Row prior to his incarceration, stating matter-of-factly that "I have no regrets… Where God puts a period, ain't no man can put a question mark. I guess God kept me in five years because he felt I had a lot to learn. And I did."

The media, in their ever-paradoxical style, has both celebrated Knight's release for the notoriety and controversy. It instantly inspires (i.e. papers it sells), and in the same time, openly doubts Death Row's real chances at anything beyond a novelty comeback. Notably exemplified in a tabloid-esque article that was picked up by both the *New York Times* and AOL *Entertainment Wire*, entitled "*SUGE KNIGHT FACES TOUGH ROW TO HOE*". Wrought with the sort of negative speculation that often pollutes the twenty first century definition of objective reporting, the article, at one point, questions the label's real chances for future successes, pointing to the fact that its hits during Knight's incarceration came via unreleased material recorded years earlier, such that the reporter questioned whether the trend could "translate into a new string of hits with Knight back at the helm", concluding that the answer was "still far from certain."

The answer to the aforementioned speculation largely lies with Suge alone. Where the same media journalists who had four years earlier pronounced the eminent end of Death Row's reign at the forefront of rap at the news of Knight's incarceration, they now had, for the entirety of the Spring of 2000, peppered Suge with enthusiastic questions about his plans for Death Row upon release from prison. They did so, in part, because the label had survived, largely contrary to the press's forecasts and predictions.

For Suge, it was all sunshine, not only because had be planned well in advance of his incarceration with the insurance of control over hundreds of unreleased Master recordings from artists like Tupac and Snoop Dogg, but because he did not thrive, as the media did, on the negativity his prison sentence inspired. Rather than indulge their suspect objectivity, Suge chose to quash it with his own objectivity concerning the future, concluding that "the past is the past, and one thing about Death Row Records is it's youthful...The plan is to move forward and give opportunities and deals to those young artists out there... My plan is just to come out and do positive things but to have fun with it—really go back to the hard-working days of putting out great records and movies." In truth, the challenge had been Suge's alone, and he had handled it like a man. He had accomplished this by admitting his role in the circumstances that had led to his incarceration, doing his time like a soldier, and forcing himself to grow from the experience. In an interview conducted in the summer of 2001, Suge reflected on the latter, remarking to a journalist that "I'm smarter now. Only thing separating me from the game right now is that I'm in prison. But I've done my time, held my head up, and now I'm on my way home." Indeed he was.

What becomes of Death Row Records is now a matter squarely in Knight's court, with Big Suge sitting up in the judge's bench. His iron hammer might have lost some of its polish, but no doubt is still hot, and ready to strike again. As one music industry executive, Russell Simmon's business partner of 17 years, Lyor Cohen, President of Def Jam Records, commented regarding Death Row's long-term viability in a *Newsweek* feature on Suge's coming release in May, 2001, "Suge knows talent, he knows his music, and that and the money are what count in this industry." Knight had given an almost identical answer eight years earlier in a feature on Death Row as an upcoming label with a violent business-tact reputation, "As long as you got money coming in, (the industry) will deal with you." In answering questions today regarding whether Death Row will again seek a corporate partner in its quest to regain rap's championship belt, Suge has remained largely silent, preferring to let time tell the story of Death Row's second coming. As Tupac had rhymed prophetically in the #1 hit from Death Row's spring 2001 Shakur from-the-grave release *Until the End of Time,*

> "Now who's to say if I was right or wrong?
> To live my life as an Outlaw all along,
> Remain strong in this planet full of player haters,
> They conversate but Death Row full of demonstrators...
> Another album out, that's what I'm about, more...
> Gettin' raw 'til the day I see my casket...
> Buried as a G while the whole world remembers me...
> Until the end of time"

In the spirit of his departed brother, Suge has a lot to live for. Fulfilling Tupac's dreams, as well as seeing his own through with respect to Death Row's place in Hip Hop's Hall of Fame, raising the sagging West Coast sun up to shine again at the forefront of hip hop, giving back to the community that kept him going on the inside, and being true to himself as a man with respect to what Knight's ulti-mate legacy will be. Will he be eventually grouped in with the likes of Morris Levy and other old school, payola honchos as a cheat who left his artists out in the cold upon being incarcerated? Or will Knight be remembered historically as a captain who stayed loyally on board his ship while the majority of his crew jumped over board when the tides turned against him?

Ultimately, Knight has stayed afloat, and largely balanced through a combination of savvy business foresight and inner peace achieved through a brutally-honest period of reflection. To that end, in many ways, Knight seems resolved that prison may have been the best thing for him at the time he was initially incarcerated, where in retro-spect, "(prison) was a learning experience. It was some-thing I definitely needed because it made me a smarter, stronger, better man." In answering questions about his label's handling of its marquee artists, Suge has called the deals many of them had when signed to white-owned labels prior to joining Death Row's African Ameri-can-themed, owned, and operated roster "contracts...like the days of Chuck Berry and Little Richard, when the acts had to tap-dance for a deal, like strippers with $20 in their G-string." In commenting on the allegations that he cheated his artists, Suge has traditionally taken a more defensive stance, refuting the notion that his artists losing money with the label was on him, but rather that "of all the artists on Death Row, none of them went bankrupt. They was having chips and cars and all that. Now, if they fuck theirs off, then that's on them."

Ultimately, Suge seems more intent on settling Death Row's position in today's hip hop mainstream as some-thing similar to that of a Godfather's, wherein "People can act like the Death Row concept is over, but to be successful, you have to follow the format we established...Today's gangsta hip-hop isn't real if it doesn't follow the guidelines we set at Death Row." He has expressed strong opinions on the current crop of hip hop's hottest artists, principally concentrated in the East Coast, as a group that, in some instances, he is a fan of, but collectively he clearly feels has benefited from Death Row's absence, such that "I think Jay-Z benefited from that fact that 'Pac and Biggie are dead. When they were around, he wasn't on that level. What I do like about DMX—even though people say he bit 'Pac's style—is that he has a great work ethic. I like them Ruff Ryder niggas. They real ghetto niggas, rappin." An important part of any legacy Suge will historically hold will also depend on the next generation of Death Row superstars he is able to produce for the record buying masses. Today, Death Row's roster consists of a crop of up and comers that Knight describes by the declaration that "my immediate plan is to give opportunities back to the inner city, back to the ghetto...I feel rap and hip-hop are a young man's game...Those kids in the ghetto who are really living that life and writing those rhymes—its time for them to get their chance to take care of their family and get them out of the ghetto. I'm that man who believes in giving opportunities. My main goal is to go searching for not only Death Row's next star, but the world's next star. Because it's time."

When reflecting on Death Row's super stars of yesteryear, Knight's roster speaks for itself. While he has had public beefs with Dr. Dre, the Dogg Pound, and most notably, Snoop Dogg, the one Death Row inmate who has never left Knight's mind, or in many ways, his heart, is Tupac. Inseparable from the moment Knight sprung him from prison in October, 1995, Suge Knight is permanently engrained in any hip hop fan's memory of Tupac, both because he was at his most prolific while recording for Death Row, and because he and Knight were clearly kindred spirits. Equally, Tupac will be forever etched in Suge's mind as his little brother. Just as the last picture ever taken of Tupac alive on the night of September 7 reflects, Suge was Tupac's keeper, the shadow of his ever-vibrant light, and as both Suge and Pac have readily referred to the other, soul mates. In reflecting on he and Tupac's time together, Suge clearly feels it was not measured by the constraints of hours or days, as though it was only eight months, the energy they collectively generated within Hip Hop and legacy they accomplished together would have taken most artists, at their most prolific, an entire career to affect. What Suge and Pac attained, in commercial success and personal friendship, is timeless.

In retrospect, it seems important, however, for Suge to focus on their aforementioned kinship over any commercial heights in terms of a long term perspective on Tupac and Death Row, reflecting that "I lost a lot of loved ones like him. If you around me then I have your back. I never make no fake ass records talking about 'Pac like Puffy did 'Missing You.' He did that to benefit himself. (Pac) was my nigga and I will never do no record like that. People talk about that shit, but can't nobody say me and Pac didn't have fun." It seems now time for *Big Suge* to take care of his business, with a renewed sense of vigor and an edge, rooted very much in what promises to be a more stable period for Death Row's rebirth. As the next generation of stars line up for a spot on Death Row's roster, Suge Knight could very well be responsible for the next renaissance of West Coast hip hop. Still, no one can truely predict Death Row's real potential for success, as Suge himself is still going through the motions of realizing its possibility, "I'd say its gotta be really indescribable to know that you're actually walking away from prison walls and little bitty cells. There's nothing better than knowing you're walking to freedom."

Author Biography

Jake Brown resides in New York and is President of Versailles Records. An avid writer, he has penned several books, including: *An Education In Rebellion: The Biography of Nikki Sixx, Guilty Till Proven Innocent: The King of New York: The Biography of Notorious B.I.G., Inside the Lion's Den: The Authorized Biography of Shelly Finkel.*